THE
ETERNAL
DRAMA

THE

The Inner Meaning

EDWARD F. EDINGER

ETERNAL
DRAMA

of Greek Mythology

Edited by
DEBORAH A. WESLEY

SHAMBHALA
BOSTON & LONDON
1994

Shambhala Publications, Inc.
Horticultural Hall
300 Massachusetts Avenue
Boston, Massachusetts 02115

9 8 7 6 5 4 3 2 1

First Edition

Designed by Dede Cummings

Printed in the United States of America on acid-free paper ⊗

Distributed in the United States by Random House, Inc.,
and in Canada by Random House of Canada Ltd

Library of Congress Cataloging-in-Publication Data

Edinger, Edward F.
    The eternal drama: the inner meaning of Greek mythology/
    Edward F. Edinger; edited by Deborah A. Wesley.—1st ed.
        p. cm.
    Includes bibliographical references and index.
    ISBN 0-87773-989-7 (pbk.: alk. paper)
    1. Mythology, Greek—Psychological aspects.
    2. Psychoanalysis.
    I. Wesley, Deborah A.   II. Title.
    BF175.5.M95E35   1994   94-8331
    292.1′3′019—dc20   CIP

Contents

Illustrations

Author's Note

I WANT to thank the editor, Deborah Wesley, warmly for her successful efforts to transform rough and scattered material into a relatively smooth and unified whole. Jung said that "any renewal not deeply rooted in the best spiritual tradition is ephemeral." Greek mythology is the foundation of one part of our "best spiritual tradition," and Jung has given us the means to assimilate this rich storehouse of archetypal imagery to the modern mind. May this book contribute to that goal.

Editor's Preface

THIS TEXT brings into written form for the first time Edward F. Edinger's discussion of the psychological meanings to be found in Greek mythology, epic, drama, and religious practice. Presented in the 1970s as two series of lectures, one in New York City and one in California, the material shows the author mining the ore of Greek culture for the gold of psychological insight useful to modern individuals.

In the almost twenty years since the lectures were presented, Dr. Edinger, a noted psychiatrist and Jungian analyst, has brought forth books on the psychological dimensions of medieval alchemy, the Old and New Testaments, Melville's *Moby-Dick,* and Goethe's *Faust,* and he has spoken and written in explication of a number of C. G. Jung's later works. Throughout his writings, as in these lectures, he expresses his indebtedness to the seminal thinking of Jung, and carries Jung's ideas into fresh areas of thought and application.

Both Jung and Edinger have sought new understanding of the deep layers of the human psyche by burrowing into wide-ranging cultural contexts. This burrowing, motivated by the search for psychological insight rather than for scholarly learning in any specific cultural field, has been described by Edinger as "poaching": "We [Jungian psychologists] are constantly venturing into scholarly realms of history and anthropology and mythology—all the arts—tracking our prey . . . the psyche."[1] Here, the territory broached belongs more conventionally to the classicist, yet in the hands of this expert tracker yields bountiful psychological material.

Readers may find that the broad scope of Edinger's survey leaves them wishing for more material, a fuller development, and more discussion of the basic texts. Our hope in bringing the lectures to a wider audience is that readers may be led into their own exploration and imaginative musing on the meanings in the old stories, seeking their own connections to them.

The text of this book is a recasting of the original lectures and of an essay, "The Tragic Hero: An Image of Individuation," which originally appeared in the journal *Parabola*.[2] The Greek myths have come down to us in widely variant forms; the versions used here are for the most part those to be found in Robert Graves's *The Greek Myths*.

I want to thank Thornton Ladd, whose idea started this project, and who has been a creative collaborator from first to last—the book is really a joint venture. The volume owes much as well to my husband, David Wesley, who acted as my editorial mentor and assisted generously in the editorial work. I am also grateful to George Elder, who brought the material of the New York lectures to my attention and continued with encouragement and helpful editorial advice. Further thanks are due Professor Douglas Domingo-Forasté of the California State University, Long Beach, who provided many scholarly suggestions, and to David O'Neal of Shambhala Publications. Finally, I thank Lyn La Cava, whose transcript of the original lectures sponsored by the C. G. Jung Institute of San Francisco preserved the material through all these years and provided the basis for this text.

Deborah A. Wesley

THE
ETERNAL
DRAMA

1

What Is Mythology?

WHAT IS mythology? There are almost as many answers to this question as there are different human standpoints. On the broadest level, we can say that a people sharing a system of religious belief has a common myth. In this sense, a myth expresses metaphysical truths and gives answers to the basic questions of life. What we see more commonly today are conceptions of mythology that differ according to the field of thought from which they arise. By scientists mythology is often seen as a primitive effort to give explanations of nature—in short, as just inferior science. Philosphers and theologians tend to think of it as primitive philosophy or religion. The historically oriented read the great stories as the half-forgotten deposit of historical happenings that are left in the folk mind in the form of myth. Anthropologists and sociologists see myths as describing changes in social structures. For artists and poets, mythology is a treasury of images to be used in their craft, a common coin of the imagination for re-minting into new forms.

Although a case can be made for each of these conceptions, there is now an understanding of mythology that incorporates all these partial explanations and describes myth as it can be understood by the modern mind. This is the psychological view of C. G. Jung, which can be summarized by saying that mythology is the self-revelation of the archetypal psyche. Jung conceived of the human psyche as consisting of two interpenetrating levels, the personal and the archetypal (or transpersonal). The personal level derives from the immediate experience of one's own life history. The deeper, archetypal level does not have its source in personal experience, but is an innate psychological structure, present at birth and common to all human beings just as the physical structure of the body is. This inner structure is composed of the archetypes, universal patterns representing the typical experiences of mankind. The archetypal level is revealed in religions, the arts, in the fruits of human creativity, and in dreams and visions. Jung suggests that mythology, too, arises from this nonpersonal layer of the human psyche. In the myths we find particular forms and images through which we can grasp the archetypal realities that underlie all psychic experience and to a large extent determine it. From this it can be seen that a knowledge of the mythological layers is instrumental in our becoming aware of the deep levels of the psyche.

Jung recognized that mythological images give us ways of understanding the archetypal dimension. If the conscious mind does not contain such categories of understanding—religious concepts, mythological concepts—it will have no bridge to the deeper psychic layers. In such a case, the conscious mind will either be totally alienated from its psychic depths or it will be identified with them. Without a conception of God, for example, we are apt to behave as though we were God ourselves. Of course, this would not be a conscious thought, but in behavior and reactivity the ego is likely to identify with the very thing that it has no way to conceive of—in this case, divinity. And the category of divinity—the gods—is what myths tell us about.

Why should we study mythology? As we reflect on the mythological images, we are studying the facts of the psyche and trying to interpret them. Some of these interpretations are fallible, of course, but the facts are not. The facts, the mythological images themselves, have a reality that transcends interpretation. As we consider the basic images of Greek mythology, we should ask what the particular images could mean in our own individual lives. It is important to read the myths psychologically, to connect them with living experience so that they are not just remote abstractions.

A specific technique can help to do that. With every myth, one can bring personal associations to each figure and image, just as in dealing with a dream. When Heracles is condemned to serve Eurystheus or Omphale (he is forced into a life of perpetual service) the question must be asked: "How have I had an experience like this one, where tasks have been imposed upon me, that parallels this myth?" Asking such questions feeds the unconscious and is apt to draw up an association—a thought or memory. By paying attention to these associations one will start to build a personal connection to the myth; particular myths, at least, will be living themselves out in one's own life. Asking these questions will be rewarded every now and then by a shock of recognition that says: "This is my myth. This is myself I am seeing here."

The Greek myths are sacred scripture, no less than the Hebrew Bible and the New Testament. Certainly the Greek myths and what was built on them—the science and philosophy and literature—form some of the basic roots of the Western unconscious. Myths are not simply tales of happenings in the remote past but eternal dramas that are living themselves out repeatedly in our own personal lives and in what we see all around us. To be aware of this adds a dimension to existence that is usually reserved for the poets. To the extent that we can cultivate awareness of this transpersonal dimension, life is enlarged and broadened. Just as Moses is eternally bringing down the law and Jesus is forever being crucified and resurrected, so Heracles is eternally performing his labors, Perseus is still confronting Medusa, and Theseus is forever stalking the Minotaur. All these dramas are happening in us and around us constantly. They are eternal patterns of the way life happens below the surface, if only one can see it.

While myths can lead us to a comprehension of the larger dimensions of our being, an understanding of myths can teach us as well what we are not. Jung tells us:

> The libido that will not flow into life at the right time regresses to the mythical world of the archetypes, where it activates images which, since the remotest times, have expressed the non-human life of the gods, whether of the upper world or the lower. If this regression occurs in a young person, his own individual life is supplanted by the divine archetypal drama, which is all the more devastating for him because his conscious education provides him with no means of recognizing what is happening, and thus with no possibility of freeing himself from its fascination. Herein lay the vital importance of myths: they explained to the bewildered human being what was going on in his unconscious and why he was held fast. The myths told him: "This is not you but the gods. You will never reach them, so turn back to your human avocations, holding the gods in fear and respect."[1]

Jung is referring to the danger of falling into grandiose identification with the archetypal images, which in its extreme form is psychosis. Knowing that the gods exist makes one less likely to mistake oneself for a god. In this way myths help tell the ego what it is not. As we shall see in the discussion of the Perseus myth, the whole body of mythology can be thought of as an example of Athena's mirror shield, which enabled Perseus to deal with Medusa. By reflecting it, mythology enables us to get some grasp of the transpersonal dimension, which otherwise would be overwhelming in its raw primordial power.

Where do myths come from? The psychological view is that they emerge progressively from the collective unconscious and gradually, by the collective endeavor of the race, are worked over and embodied in some durable form. But from almost the beginning this question has come up: do they not rather express the residue of some historical reality? Archeological studies suggest that there may indeed have been a Trojan war—which wasn't known a few hundred years ago. We also find some parallels to the labyrinth and the bull combat of the Theseus myth, in Crete. The historical aspect of myth needs some attention. As far back as the third or fourth century BC, a man named

Euhemerus put forth the idea that myths are all derived from historical happenings, and that all heroes, for instance, were once actual kings or actual historical personages. This later developed into a reductive theory that took all the glory out of mythology. That euhemeristic idea has not died. It comes up again and again, for example in Robert Graves's commentaries on myths.[2]

It is an indisputable fact that certain myths, and for all we know maybe all of them, had some historical origin or root. Certainly it is widely believed that the Christian myth derived from an actual historical personage. One observes that certain historical experiences, when they illustrate some basic and universal feature of the human psyche, turn into myth. So there is an interchange between history and archetype. For example, one can speculate on what might happen if there were a gap in all our records for a few hundred years and historians of 2500 AD were to look at the fact that Abraham Lincoln was assassinated on Good Friday. Would they believe that as a simple fact, or would they say, "Well, isn't that interesting. Here is this historical figure who we know existed, but he was so quickly assimilated into the Christian myth that they couldn't make the distinction between who Lincoln was and who Christ was"? We, of course, know that he actually was shot on Good Friday, but would a future historian accept that, if the records were lost? Perhaps not.

So there is a true mystery as to just how the overlap and interchange take place between the historical process that individual egos live out and the archetypal dimension, which sometimes determines the drama of the ego and at other times seems to be influenced in its manifestation by the way the ego lives its life. For example, in *The Iliad* at one point Helen says to Hector that Zeus has given them a hard fate so that thereafter they may be the subject of a "future song for men."[3] What she is saying, in a sense, is that we have to live our hard fate now because we are destined to exemplify an archetypal image for future man.

Another aspect of that same issue is a question about how the ego might contribute to the unfolding, development, and enlarged manifestation of the archetypal world. A great man's hunger for fame and immortality can often be understood as the longing to fulfill his fate of augmenting archetypal imagery. In his poem "Lycidas," Milton speaks of this yearning, quite explicitly and beautifully, as determined not by the ego, but by the transpersonal powers:

> Fame is the spur that the clear spirit doth raise
> (That last infirmity of noble mind)
> To scorn delights, and live laborious days;
> But the fair guerdon when we hope to find,
> And think to burst out into sudden blaze,
> Comes the blind fury with the abhorred shears,
> And slits the thinspun life. "But not the praise,"
> Phoebus replied, and touched my trembling ears:

He is talking about fame and praise, just petty ego ambition presumably. But here Milton makes his point:

> "Fame is no plant that grows on mortal soil,
> Nor in the glistering foil
> Set off to th' world, nor in broad rumor lies,
> But lives and spreads aloft by those pure eyes,
> And perfect witness of all-judging Jove;
> As he pronounces lastly on each deed,
> Of so much fame in Heaven expect thy meed."[4]

That is an example of how what we might call the power motive, if perceived in a personalistic framework, turns into a completely different thing if understood in the larger context of one's life opus.

Another reason for studying mythology is expressed by Keats. Everybody knows the first few lines of "Endymion." It is a mythological poem, and the familiar opening lines are really an expression of Keats's feeling about myths.

> A thing of beauty is a joy forever:
> Its loveliness increases; it will never
> Pass into nothingness; but still will keep
> A bower quiet for us, and a sleep

Full of sweet dreams, and health, and quiet breathing.
Therefore, on every morrow, are we wreathing
A flowery band to bind us to the earth.
Spite of despondence, of the inhuman dearth
Of noble natures, of the gloomy days,
Of all the unhealthy and o'er-darkened ways
Made for our searching: yes, in spite of all,
Some shape of beauty moves away the pall
From our dark spirits. Such the sun, the moon,
Trees old and young, sprouting a shady boon
For simple sheep; and such are daffodils
With the green world they live in, and clear rills
That for themselves a cooling covert make
'Gainst the hot season; the mid-forest brake,
Rich with a sprinkling of fair musk-rose blooms.

Now here is his description of myth:

And such too is the grandeur of the dooms
We have imagined for the mighty dead;
All lovely tales that we have heard or read:
An endless fountain of immortal drink,
Pouring unto us from the heaven's brink.[5]

Of course poets know all about this spiritual nourishment because they are all mythologists. They make the mythical images visible. They live in a constant awareness of the archetypal powers. Theodore Dreiser, a literary man who had something of a poet in him, gave an impeccable psychological description of the reality of a mythical image when he said that he knew that the Furies existed because he had heard the beating of their wings.

A final reason for studying mythology is expressed in the Baucis and Philemon myth. The story is that the gods Zeus and Hermes came to earth looking for a devout man. They took the form of travelers and wandered about seeking hospitality. No one would let them in until they came to the poor hut of a pious old couple, Baucis and

Philemon, who brought out all they had and fed and took care of them. Then a flood came and only Baucis and Philemon were saved. Their wish to be guardians of the gods' temple was granted. According to Ovid, who tells the story, the moral is (and it is not badly put): "The gods look after good people still, and cherishers are cherished."[6] That corresponds to what has been discovered in depth psychology, that when one pays attention to the unconscious, the unconscious is likely to show some kindness to the ego that does so. The cherishers are cherished. The Baucis and Philemon myth expresses a good reason for studying mythology. It is like entertaining Zeus and Hermes, letting them in and giving them whatever we have to offer. It is good for the soul.

2

The
Beginnings

COSMOGONY

A CONSIDERATION of Greek mythology must start with at least a brief look at the myths of creation or cosmogony. There are several versions of how the cosmos came into existence. The simplest is that first there was Chaos, and out of Chaos earth, or Gaia, emerged. Gaia gave birth to the sky, or Uranus, and then Gaia and Uranus produced a great progeny. So from Chaos a pair of world parents emerged and separated, who then created all the rest that exists. What would that mean psychologically? For one thing it is an image of how the personality or the prefigurations of the ego (we can't speak of the ego yet) first begin. One can also think of it as representing how each new bit of psyche is created. After all, it is a creation myth, and it does fit our psychological experience that the creative act itself involves exposure to chaos. Creation means that something new comes into the world that did not previously exist. And if so, from whence does it come? The only place it can come from is the void region of nonbeing characterized in the myth as

Chaos. That is the womb, the unbegotten womb of all things yet to be, and hence the experience of creativity commonly has as a forerunner or an accompaniment the experience of chaos. Nothing new can emerge unless one is willing to dip into chaos and pull it out.

Once it is out, it promptly splits into two, into earth and sky in terms of the myth. This is something we see whenever something is coming into awareness: the very process of achieving consciousness involves a split into opposites. Things can remain in their state of oneness only as long as they are unconscious. When they reach consciousness, they must divide into opposites and then we have the experience of conflict. When things are seen in twos in dreams, there is the suggestion that they are achieving a conscious status for the first time.

The myths tell us that Uranus and Gaia were the first king and queen in the divine kingdom. There were wars for the kingship, and a series of dethronements took place in this very early mythology. The king did not want to let anything survive that was threatening to him, so he took certain repressive measures, which then called forth counteractions. These early dethronements, can be thought of psychologically. Humankind had not yet appeared at this stage of the story; hence, if we take the human being to signify the ego, the ego did not really exist. These ancient deities can be seen as prefigurations of the ego or as the primordial Self* in conjunction with the ego germ. They were undergoing a certain transformative evolution, signified by the early dethronements.

Uranus got into trouble because he imprisoned certain of his children. The two major branches of his offspring were the Titans on the one hand, and the Cyclopes on the other. The Cyclopes, giants that had a central round eye—the word means "wheel eye" literally— were confined in the earth. Upset at Uranus' imprisonment of them, the mother, always the more merciful of the two parents, stirred up her son Kronos to revolt against Uranus. Kronos lay in wait for him and castrated him; the drops of blood that fell on the earth generated the Erinyes, the Furies, and the genitals fell into the sea and are said

*For a definition of *Self,* see the glossary.

to have given rise to Aphrodite. One could say that the Cyclopes, since they were characterized primarily by their one round eye, represent a psychic aspect that has not split into doubleness. The roundness suggests a certain primordial wholeness that was being repressed by Uranus. The consequences of Uranus' castration might be thought of as the birth of desire (Aphrodite) and the birth of punishment (the Erinyes).

The castration of Uranus was taken by Freud as a mythological example of the castration complex, the son wanting to supplant the father and in effect castrate him but fearing like treatment from the father. The episode can also be thought of in a more general sense. In the case of both Uranus and Kronos, a principle that is in power seeks to perpetuate itself and to eliminate all threats to its authority. This is an image of what can happen within the psyche: an old principle must die if development is to proceed, and it has to be overcome by the emerging new principle itself. That was the case with Uranus, and it happened as well when Kronos, who succeeded him, behaved no better. It was prophesied that Kronos might be deposed by one of his offspring; he reacted by swallowing all his children—a primordial version of the devouring parent, an image universally encountered. Ultimately Kronos, a Titan, was cast out in a war between the gods and the Titans and was replaced by Zeus, who belonged to the race of the gods. A whole dynasty of psychic authorities was being overthrown and replaced by a new one. There was a real *Götterdämmerung* in the ancient Pantheon.

The Titans who were vanquished served some very useful purposes. Two outstanding ones were Atlas and Prometheus. Atlas' punishment for losing the war, so to speak, was to be condemned to hold up the earth, which he has been doing ever since. In a certain sense, the Titans became sacrifices for humankind's well-being. The archetypal contents that they represent went into the service of the ego.

The primary example of this is the story of Prometheus. Even though the Titans had lost the war, Prometheus was still present and still against the gods, and at that stage opposing the gods meant being on the side of humanity. Prometheus' story begins when he was assigned to supervise the separation of the sacrificial meat to determine

FIG. 1. The War of the Gods and the Titans. Just right of center, Zeus mounts his chariot in which Heracles stands with a drawn bow, while Gaia pleads for the life of her children, the Titans. Behind him, Hermes with his

which part went to the gods and which to humankind. Previously, gods and humans had eaten together, but now they were to eat apart, signifying a separation of the ego from its archetypal origins. Prometheus deceived the gods by wrapping up bones and skin for them in a very enticing package and leaving all the nourishing meat for humankind. In punishment for this, Zeus deprived humanity of fire. Prometheus proceeded to steal it for the benefit of humankind, and for that crime he was chained in the Caucasus Mountains. There, his liver was eaten away each day by a vulture, but the wound would heal each night. In this way, the process repeated endlessly.

Prometheus' story gives us profound images of the nature of emerging consciousness. First there is the process of separation, which determines what belongs to the gods and what belongs to humankind, the ego gaining increments of meat, or energy, for itself. Then humanity is provided with fire, one could say with light and energy: consciousness and the effective energy of will to carry out conscious intention are created. However, there was a fearful price for this, because the acquisition of consciousness was a crime, as described in the myth, and its consequence was to generate in Prometheus an unhealing wound, the wound inflicted by the vulture by day—during the time of light and consciousness. This particular detail indicates that consciousness itself is the vulture, the wound-producer. Prometheus pays for the consciousness of humanity with

Gorgon Shield and Dionysus assisted by lions, panthers, and a snake, battle the Titans. (From a reconstruction by M. Moore of an Attic dinos, c. 560 BC. Transcription by J. Wheelock.)

his suffering, much like Christ. As a Titan, he belongs to the divine realm; he is not human but an archetypal or non-ego factor, which so loved humankind that it put itself in humanity's service, that is, in the service of the ego, in order to promote its development.

The image of Prometheus has fascinated the poets and led them to identify with him—a dangerous identification. Goethe was one. He declared, "The fable of Prometheus came alive in me. I cut the old Titan rope to my own size." Shelley and Byron were both preoccupied with the image of Prometheus. Longfellow has some lines in his poem "Prometheus" that express a quite widespread feeling about the Promethean quality in the creative artist:

First the deed of noble daring,
Born of heavenward aspiration,
Then the fire with mortals sharing,
Then the vulture—the despairing
Cry of pain on crags Caucasian.

All is but a symbol painted
Of the Poet, Prophet, Seer;
Only those are crowned and sainted
Who with grief have been acquainted,
Making nations nobler, freer.

FIG. 2. Atlas and Prometheus. Atlas is shown holding up the heavens. His brother Prometheus is
bound and attacked by a vulture in punishment for
aiding mankind. (Detail of a Laconian cylix, c. 560 BC.
Vatican Museum, Rome. Photo: Alinari/Art Resource,
New York.)

In their feverish exultations,
In their triumph and their yearning,
In their passionate pulsations,
In their words among the nations,
The Promethean fire is burning. . . .

Though to all there be not given
Strength for such sublime endeavor,
Thus to scale the walls of heaven,
And to leaven with fiery leaven,
All the hearts of men forever;

Yet all bards, whose hearts unblighted
Honor and believe the presage,
Hold aloft their torches lighted,

Gleaming through the realms benighted,
As they onward bear the message![1]

Another consequence of Prometheus' acts was the punishment meted out to his brother Epimetheus, who can be thought of as a variant of Prometheus. He received the gift of Pandora. In a certain sense we could say that Pandora and fire are equivalent. Fire is energy and one of the aspects of energy is desire: Pandora, the beautiful woman, is the object of desire. As the ego is given the powers of desire and will and longing, it also receives the contents of Pandora's box, the sufferings of human life. This is a very close parallel with the myth of Adam and Eve. Both signify the painful aspect of being born into egohood. As these myths describe it, the unconscious state is paradise and the birth of the ego is paid for by suffering.

Aeschylus' *Prometheus Bound* pictures how Prometheus was regarded by the Greeks of the fifth century BC. He was a culture hero and hence we can say he was the incarnation of the consciousness-bringing principle itself. In Aeschylus' play, Prometheus says:

[L]isten to the sad story of mankind, who like children lived until I gave them understanding and a portion of reason; yet not in disparagement of men I speak, but meaning to set forth the greatness of my charity. For seeing they saw not, and hearing they understood not, but like as shapes in a dream they wrought all the days of their life in confusion. No houses of brick raised in the warmth of the sun they had, nor fabrics of wood, but like the little ants they dwelt underground in the sunless depths of caverns. No certain sign of approaching winter they knew, no harbinger of flowering spring or fruitful summer; ever they labored at random, till I taught them to discern the seasons by the rising and the obscure setting of the stars. Numbers I invented for them, the chiefest of all discoveries; I taught them the grouping of letters, to be a memorial and record of the past, the mistress of the arts and mother of the Muses. I first brought under the yoke beasts of burden, who by draft and carrying relieved men of their hardest labors; I yoked the proud horse to the chariot, teaching him obedience to the reins, to be the adornment of wealth and luxury. I too contrived for sailors sea-faring vessels with their flaxen wings. . . .

If sickness visited them, they had no healing drug, no salve or soothing potion, but wasted away for want of remedies, and this was my
greatest boon; for I revealed to them the mingling of bland medica-
ments for the banishing of all diseases. And many modes of divination
I appointed: from dreams I first taught them to judge what should
befall in waking state; I found the subtle interpretation of words half
heard or heard by chance, and of meetings by the way; and the flight
of taloned birds with their promise of fortune or failure I clearly de-
noted, their various modes of life, their mutual feuds, their friendships
and consortings; . . . And the secret treasures of the earth, all benefits
to men, copper, iron, silver, gold—who but I could boast of their discovery? . . . Nay, hear the whole matter in a word—all human arts are
from Prometheus.[2]

He was the bringer of consciousness. Although many figures carry
this quality, Prometheus must have been profoundly meaningful to
the ancient Greeks, to be described in this way by their chief dram-
atist.

The parallel to Christ is obvious. There are also similarities to the
Biblical "suffering servant" passage in Isaiah, except that Prometheus is defiant, where the suffering servant is described as meek. We
read in Isaiah this description of the suffering servant of God:

He grew up before the Lord like a young plant
whose roots are in parched ground;
he had no beauty, no majesty to draw our eyes,
no grace to make us delight in him;
his form, disfigured, lost all the likeness of a man,
his beauty changed beyond human semblance.
He was despised, he shrank from the sight of men,
tormented and humbled by suffering;
we despised him, we held him of no account,
a thing from which men turn away their eyes.
Yet on himself he bore our sufferings,
our torments he endured,
while we counted him smitten by God,
struck down by disease and misery;

but he was pierced for our transgressions,
tortured for our iniquities;
the chastisement he bore is health for us
and by his scourging we are healed.
We had all strayed like sheep,
each of us had gone his own way;
but the Lord laid upon him
the guilt of us all.[3]

This clearly echoes the story of Prometheus. Surely it is significant that a basically similar figure appears in each of our three major scriptural sources, the Greek, Hebrew, and Christian. The psychological meaning is difficult to encompass, but two aspects seem clear. One is that consciousness is accompanied by suffering, and the other is that the ego does not have to do all the suffering. There is an archetypal advocate or benefactor that supports and assists the ego. Whether we call him the suffering servant of Isaiah or Prometheus or Christ, there is an advocate in the archetypal realm. Prometheus is perhaps the first and one of the finest expressions of this archetypal fact.

3

The Olympian Gods

I T I S remarkable that the early civilized mind took it as self-evident that there were beings who lived forever. This is not so obvious to the modern mind; one has to dig into the depths of psychological experience to rediscover what was self-evident to our ancestors. Taken as a whole, the Greek Pantheon tells us that the immortal ones are fundamental presences. In psychological terms, we can say that they are inhabitants of the collective unconscious. They are expressions of the archetypes, those psychic entities that continue to exist unchanging while the momentary individual egos come and go.

One of the striking features of *The Iliad* is that gods and men are active on the same stage. In the course of the battles and the to-and-fro of the champions and the warriors and armies, not only are there human soldiers on the field, but gods are there fighting along with them. Every now and then one of the gods will take one particular warrior and imbue him with superior power, or if a favorite is having a bad time of it, he may just pick him up bodily in a cloud and transport him to safety. If we take this as a picture of the psychological realm, we see that there is a free, fluid interpenetration between ego experience and archetypal factors signified by the gods. The nature of psychological experience is that what we do and what we experience are constantly interpenetrated by these other powers, although as a rule consciousness is making so much noise, it doesn't notice.

The fact that there are twelve Olympians is surely significant—although the roster is not absolutely fixed; there were some late revisions. Dionysus is a late addition, and Demeter is not always present. However, it seems important to point out in a general way the symbolism of the sacred number twelve. One need only think of the twelve hours of the day, the twelve tribes of Israel, the twelve apostles of Christ, the twelve signs of the zodiac, the twelve labors of Heracles. Twelve is related to the symbolism of wholeness, to the mandala and the quaternity. It is a particularly meaningful number for the sacred ones. As the ego looks in the direction of the Self, the transpersonal center of the psyche, it tends to experience the Self not as a unity (at least not at first) but as a multiplicity of archetypal factors that one can think of as the Greek gods.

Let us consider the gods as a whole before discussing the individuals. From the viewpoint of depth psychology, the gods stand for the archetypes, the basic patterns within the human psyche that exist independent of personal experience. They are the templates on which the individual life is formed. Mythologically, these eternal patterns are thought of as gods, existing in a special place apart from ordinary human experience. The Greeks called that special region Olympus, and thought of it originally as a mountain peak, and later as the whole upper sky. In *The Odyssey* Homer describes Olympus:

> . . . Olympus, where, they say, is the abode of the gods that stands fast forever. Neither is it shaken by winds or ever wet with rain, nor does snow fall upon it, but the air is outspread clear and cloudless, and over it hovers a radiant whiteness. Therein the blessed gods are glad all their days. . . .[1]

Of course, this is just one version of heaven as the transcendent realm, the realm beyond the personal. A parallel conception was the image of Yahweh in Hebrew mythology. He was also a sky god and inhabited Mount Sinai, an equivalent of Mount Olympus and analogous to the Christian heaven as well. Indeed, almost all primitive mythologies involve some notion of heaven as an abode for the gods, with something of this perfect, eternal, untarnished quality.

Psychologically we can consider the idea of an Olympian realm as a projection onto the outer world (onto the sky in this case) of an inner state. It would be a state that is eternal, unchanging, and a realm of the spirit, as opposed to matter. Every now and then one encounters the notion that such images amount to nothing more than wish fulfillment. But no wish was fulfilled in the original Greek conception of Olympus, since as the myths and all the early literature make clear, there was no advantage to them in imagining the Olympians up in their heavenly realm. Quite the contrary, the Olympian existence merely emphasized the misery of mortal life. We are left with the conclusion that there exists an eternal psyche, or something symbolized by an eternal psyche, that is of greater duration than the ego. This idea is developed in Jung's concept of the collective unconscious, the abode of the archetypes. In his purely psychological view, the heavenly realm of the Greek gods is seen as a part of the human psyche, which is beyond time and space and beyond the control of the conscious personality. The early images such as that of Olympus are understood as translations of psychological realities into external ones.

When we take the Greek gods individually, we have a complete chart of the eternal or impersonal dimension of the psyche. The assembly of the gods gives us a set of archetypal principles, along the lines that Nietzsche elaborated when he described the Dionysian and Apollonian principles in his essay "The Birth of Tragedy." The same sort of elaboration can be made for each of the Greek gods, so that we see a Zeus principle, an Ares principle, an Aphrodite principle, an Athena principle, and so on.

We experience these principles in different ways. We observe them, for instance, lived out in the personalities and behavior of others. If we review our various friends and acquaintances we can come up with examples—not in pure culture, of course, but approximate examples—of each of the archetypal principles the Greek gods embody, and we can equally well, by self-examination, detect one or more such principles that are guiding factors in our own psychology. We will encounter expressions of them in our dreams as numinous entities, having a guiding or helping capacity of some kind. The more we approach the state of wholeness, the more likely we are to have had at least brief encounters with most, if not all, of these divine principles. Each of us contains within us the whole Olympian Pantheon.

ZEUS, POSEIDON, HADES

Let us start with Zeus. He was the ultimate authority and belonged to a trinity, the paternal authority principle, which was made up of Zeus, Poseidon, and Hades. That Olympian triad can be thought of as different manifestations of the same basic principle. But Zeus is the supreme deity, and comes closest of all the members of the Pantheon to embodying the whole Self, even though he represents only the masculine side. He was a sky god, associated with wind, rain, thunder, and lightning, and was the master of spiritual phenomena, since it was the spirit realm that was signified by the sky and the manifestations of the weather. He was a carrier of justice and judgment, an embodiment of law and the punisher of transgression of the law, accomplished by the hurling of the thunderbolt. He was the personification of creative energy, which constantly spilled out and had an unceasing urge to impregnate, hence his perpetual love affairs.

It was an energy continually striving to realize new consciousness or new fruits of itself. There are long lists of the lovers of Zeus, and by and large they had an unhappy time of it. Hera, personifying the feminine embodiment of the Self, was fiercely opposed to these dalliances, and would often punish Zeus' lovers. For example, Zeus fell in love with the beautiful Io and then turned her into a white cow so that she could escape Hera's detection. This ruse failed and Hera set gadflies after her which, stinging, pursued her around the world. This was typical of Hera's jealousy, and through these images we learn

FIG. 3. Zeus holding a thunderbolt and libation cup. (Detail of an Attic cup, c. 520 BC. Museo Nazionale, Tarquinia. Photo: Nimatallah/ Art Resource, New York.)

that when the divine creative energy flows into the human realm, there is a reaction from the gods, as if there is jealousy over what has been lost to them. It appears that every gain of the ego must be paid for by punishment for having appropriated the divine energy. This psychological fact is seen many times in the consequences of Zeus' amours with mortal women. These affairs and Hera's fits of jealousy were often treated as comic relief in the sagas of the gods. However, we must remember that these are archetypal dynamisms that become the fate of human individuals, and as such can be tragic rather than comic.

We find in the image of Zeus and his lovers early forms of the same archetypal phenomenon that appears later in the Christian Annunciation: the union of the divine and the human. The Annunciation, the meeting of Mary and the Holy Ghost, appears to be a gentler encounter, yet the ultimate fate of Christ, the fruit of that union, was anything but gentle.

In these myths, we have the strange phenomenon of Zeus and Hera apparently working at cross-purposes. Zeus has the urge to create, to generate more and more offspring by different mothers in different places, and Hera's role is to resent and attempt to frustrate or somehow punish individuals who succumb to Zeus' desires. It is a little like what we see in the book of Job, where Yahweh is divided against himself; the other part of him appears as Satan. Here we see a certain ambiguity in the world of the archetypes, which are not necessarily interested in the comfort and well-being of the human ego; they may be more interested in something beyond the ego's ability to value or understand.

The imagery of Zeus can be seen to correspond closely to the first hexagram of the *I Ching,* called The Creative. The *I Ching,* the ancient Chinese oracle book, says about this hexagram, "Six unbroken lines. These unbroken lines stand for the primal power, which is light-giving, active, strong, and of the spirit. . . . Its essence is power or energy. Its image is heaven."[2] Thus we see that we are dealing here with an archetypal image that can express itself and clothe itself in multifarious ways in different cultures, but its underlying essence is the same.

How does this factor appear in psychology? It is not hard to distinguish what we might call a Zeus temperament. There are certain men—we are considering a masculine phenomenon—who are effective, self-righteous, who are embodiments of moral authority, and who are capable of casting thunderbolts at transgressors around them. They could equally well be called Yahweh temperaments, since Yahweh and Zeus are virtually interchangeable in their essential characteristics. Such a principle may also be experienced internally. If a person falls into an unconscious identification with it, he will find himself acting and reacting as though he himself were the Law, the ultimate authority. Making connection with the image objectively, rather than falling into identification with it, can lead to the capacity for objective judgment and appraisal.

An example of the Zeus phenomenon appeared in a dream of a young man who was contemplating leaving his wife and several children in order to pursue an infatuation with a young wealthy woman. Her wealth was as seductive to him as her beauty. At that point he had this dream:

> I stand in the middle of the street looking up at gray, fast-moving skies. Behind the stormy facade I catch momentary glimpses of sunny, clear weather. Apparently I am deciding some sort of trip and the weather is the important factor in the decision. On my right a group of elders are gathered in discussion. I ask them, "Do you think I should leave? The sky seems clear to me." They shake their heads collectively. I refuse the advice and I begin to walk straight toward the dark clouds. I move about two steps when the sky cracks open and a huge, brown hand reaches down, picks me up, and points me in the other direction.

There is an unusual combination of factors here, namely the weather and the sky, together with the transpersonal authority. This is precisely what the original sky god was conceived to be. He manifested himself in the weather, and that is still true today, though now we think of it as inner weather.

Zeus is the personification of law and judgment, what may be and what may not be. Those are not arbitrarily determined things, but have an objective basis in the psyche. The ego may think mistakenly that (as it was put by the antagonist in Plato's *Republic*[3]) they have no existence beyond the will of the stronger. These mythological images of moral authority indicate that human principles of law and justice, on the contrary, arise from deep within the psyche.

Poseidon is the brother of Zeus and carries something of the same quality of authority, but he signifies authority from below rather than from above. He is the lord of the sea, and earth is also his domain in that he is the earth shaker, the generator of earthquakes and tidal waves. He is an earthy version of Zeus, or God as manifested from the psychic depths or from outer circumstance. He would be felt in the impact of concrete life events that are beyond one's control.

In the *I Ching,* hexagram number 51, called The Arousing (Shock, Thunder), alludes to the Poseidon principle: "A yang line develops

FIG. 4. Poseidon with his trident rides a hippocamp (half-horse, half-fish). (Detail of an Attic lekythos, c. 490 BC. Ashmolean Museum, Oxford.)

below two yin lines and presses upward forcibly. This movement is so violent that it arouses terror. It is symbolized by thunder, which bursts forth from the earth and by its shock causes fear and trembling." We think of thunder as coming from above, but psychologically speaking, this Chinese image of thunder coming from below is entirely accurate. When one experiences an inner earthquake it is very much like thunder from below. The *I Ching* goes on to say:

The shock that comes from the manifestation of God within the depths of the earth makes man afraid, but this fear of God is good, for joy and merriment can follow upon it. . . . The superior man is always filled with reverence at the manifestation of God; he sets his life in order and searches his heart, lest it harbor any secret opposition to the will of God.[4]

Poseidon would be Zeus appearing from below. Dreams of tidal waves and earthquakes point to the activation of this principle—concrete events shaking one's foundations. The Poseidon personality would have certain similarities to the Zeus personality, but his authority and effectiveness would be more apt to manifest themselves in concrete power—political and economic—as opposed to intellectual or spiritual power.

There is less to say about Hades, the third member of this trinity. Almost the only myth that refers to him is the Demeter-Persephone story, which establishes him as an abductor to the realm of the dead.

FIG. 5. Hades holding an overflowing cornucopia, suggesting the wealth that comes out of the ground. (Detail from an Attic hydria. Copyright British Museum, London.)

So he shares with Hermes, to some extent, the position of leader into the unconscious, the Underworld. In later imagery he actually becomes a personification of death, coming to claim his victims. Another later name, Pluto, associates him with riches, so he has an ambiguous quality. It is difficult to identify a Hades personality, although a patient whose father was a mortician once described how as a little boy, when he saw the dead bodies come into his father's mortuary, he believed his father had killed them—a graphic example of the projection of the Hades figure onto the father. Certainly in inner terms Hades, who sometimes was equated with Dionysus, was thought of as the lord of the *nekyia*, the journey to the Underworld, and hence he was thought of as the ruler of the phenomenon of death and rebirth, precisely the function he served in the Demeter-Persephone story.

APOLLO

Apollo's attributes are the sun, light, clarity, truth. He represents the principle of rational consciousness which, in so many positive and heroic figures, has difficulty in being born. Hera in her jealousy pursued Apollo's mother, Leto, so that no place on earth could be found for his birth. Finally he was born on the floating island of Delos, which shows us in what tenuous ways the light of consciousness first comes into the world. No sooner did Apollo appear than the island took root, so to speak, and became solid land. That must say something about how the divine can come into being in the human realm. No firmly established ego will grant it refuge. It is allowed in where there is a more tenuous consciousness, a floating existence, which then strikes roots and becomes permanently established. One might think of certain artistic personalities as examples of this.

Apollo killed the Python of Delphi and took over that oracle, so he is a vanquisher of unconscious terrors. He is golden-haired like the sun; he is an archer who shoots arrows of insight and/or death; he is a god of music and the lyre. Healing belongs to his realm: he was the father of Asclepius, the god of medicine. The Muses are part

FIG. 6. Apollo, seated on a winged tripod, travels over the sea. (Detail of an Attic hydria, c. 480 BC. Vatican Museum, Rome. Photo: Alinari/Art Resource, New York.)

of his retinue, so that music, history, drama, poetry, dance, all belong to him. The Muses are those we call on when we evoke creative imagination to give us helpful images.

He has his ominous aspects, too. Marsyas, who dared to challenge him to a music contest, was flayed after he lost, signifying the stripping power of light. His arrows can symbolize the rays of the sun that bring light and insight but they also can bring death. *The Iliad* begins with a terrible pestilence that Apollo brought down upon the Greeks because they dishonored one of his priests. Apollo's arrows of death struck again when Queen Niobe, who was excessively proud of her seven sons and seven daughters, disparaged Apollo's mother, Leto, for having only two children. Her rash boasting brought down the wrath of Apollo and his sister, Artemis, who shot Niobe's children one by one until only a boy and a girl were left. Apollo's powerful light could be threatening in itself. He loved the nymph Daphne, but when he pursued her, she fled in terror and turned into a laurel tree to escape his embrace. In his "Hymn of Apollo," Shelley expresses the Apollonian principle well:

The sunbeams are my shafts, with which I kill
Deceit, that loves the night and fears the day:

All men, who do or even imagine ill
Fly me, and from the glory of my ray
Good minds and open actions take new might,
Until diminished by the reign of Night. . . .

I am the eye with which the Universe
Beholds itself and knows itself divine;
All harmony of instrument or verse,
All prophecy, all medicine is mine,
All light of art or nature;—to my song,
Victory and praise in its own right belong.[5]

Shelley's hymn celebrates the power and virtue of consciousness and
the capacity for truth, and the Apollonian personality would be
someone who emphasized these qualities, more or less at the expense
of the dark, Dionysian side. In inner experience, dreams that empha-
size light, illumination, fair-haired youths, would also refer to the
principle of Apollo.

HERMES

Hermes is generally portrayed with wings on his head and winged
sandals, and with a wand (the kerykeion, which later developed into
the caduceus). He is the divine messenger and hence implies something similar to what is symbolized by angels. He is a wind god and
he moves with the wind. He is the god of revelation, the bringer of
dreams, the guide of the dark way, and the psychopomp. He led souls
to the Underworld, including Orpheus when he sought Eurydice. He
was also depicted as a good shepherd, caring for the sheep, the souls
of men. The later image of Christ as the good shepherd derived from
this original image of Hermes. According to Aristophanes, he was
the friendliest of the gods to men.

In ancient Greece he was the god of boundaries. It is generally
agreed that the name Hermes is derived from the word *herm,* the
name for a pile of stones marking a boundary. But as often happens,

FIG. 7. Hermes, running, wears winged boots and carries his herald's staff. (Interior of an Attic cup, 520–510 BC. Private collection. Photo: Christies, London.)

the god of something is the one who is greater than that thing, the one who transcends it. So, though Hermes is a guarantor of boundaries in the human realm, he is the one who is beyond them. Hermes is the great trespasser, a crosser of boundaries, the god of travelers and the patron saint of merchants, the principal travelers in early days. On the darker side, he was also the patron saint of thieves—on the first day after his birth he stole Apollo's cattle. The boundary between what is mine and what is yours is one that he crosses. The Hermetic principle can deceive the Apollonian principle: Hermes does not always need to be truthful. He can be ambiguous and false and cunning, and that gets him into places that absolute light and truth and clarity could never enter.

He is a magician with a magic wand, and his ability to cross boundaries makes him a mediator between the human and the divine realm, or in psychological terms, between the personal psyche and the unconscious. He is a helper of heroes, a guide to secret regions;

some of his functions are those indicated by his name—hermeneutics, for instance, which is the science of the interpretation of the scriptures, extracting the hidden meaning. We can think of him as the patron deity of depth psychology, because depth psychology tries to relate consciousness to the unconscious depths and so repeatedly crosses the boundary between them, thus assuming the functions of Hermes.

There is always an uncanny quality about Hermes. The ancients used to say, when silence fell on a group, that Hermes had come in, as though another dimension had been tapped. We can consider him, in modern terms, as the maker of synchronicity, the bringer of unexpected coincidences, windfalls that cannot be rationally explained.

There are people who are Hermes personalities, whose guiding direction seems to be an interest in the hidden, who are carriers of secret lore, of things that are not on the surface. They tend to be expositors of the symbolical and the dark, transcenders of the ordinary boundaries of human understanding. If a person falls into an identification with the Hermetic principle, he might be compulsively obliged to convey meaning or point out hidden references, making a nuisance of himself in the process. This would be a negative identification with the principle. As the principle is encountered internally, it can serve as an objective inner guide to the unconscious. A good example was Virgil's function in *The Divine Comedy*. Virgil was Dante's Hermes, his psychopomp to the Underworld. One encounters dream figures that allude to the Hermes principle, generally winged beings who are associated with the wind and are carriers of a mediating spirit, who have one foot in each world, so to speak, and therefore can serve as guides between the two realms.

ARES

Ares was the god of war, strife, fighting. His sister Eris was the goddess of discord. Whenever she arrived on the scene, disharmony was generated, and she was the one who threw the golden apple of discord that led to the Trojan war. Ares is the principle of aggressive

FIG. 8. Ares, bearing the warrior's spear and helmet, sits with his lover, Aphrodite, who holds a dove. (Detail of an Attic cup, c. 520 BC. Museo Nazionale, Tarquinia. Photo: Soprintendenza Archaeologica per l'Etruria Meridionale.)

energy. He appears in the myths primarily as Aphrodite's lover, which shows us that the Aphrodite principle and the Ares principle have some connection. When Hephaestus, Aphrodite's cuckolded husband, heard what was going on between her and Ares, he devised a net in which he caught the lovers in the act. This might tell us that a certain kind of psychological craftsmanship can capture the raw energies of aggression and lust and bring them up to the light of consciousness.

Psychological manifestations of the Ares principle would be aggression and disputation, the kind of combativeness that is enjoyed for its own sake. It is the pugilistic attitude, the attitude of the polemicist who has more interest in the fight than in substance. It also embodies courage and the capacity for aggressive self-assertion. Professional athletes, trial lawyers, and professional soldiers would fall into this category. General George C. Patton is an outstanding example. In the movie *Patton,* which depicted his life, Patton is revealed as possessing an almost reverential attitude toward the art of war, a true worshipper at the shrine of Ares.

As an inner experience, the Ares principle emerges in situations where aggressive energy is required. Heraclitus said that war is the

father of all things,[6] and in a certain sense the willingness to fight
one's way out of original containment or out of original collective
identity is a requirement for psychological development. An example
of this principle was the dream of a man struggling with how to
approach a difficult problem in life. In the dream, a voice told him,
"It will be settled on the field of Mars." That made him realize that
he had to fight. It is interesting that the dream put the advice in an
antique format, "the field of Mars," thus pointing out that his conflict had an archetypal dimension. This gave the advice to fight a
dignity that it would not have had otherwise.

The Homeric "Hymn to Ares" was written probably around the
eighth century BC, and it is unusual in showing Ares being petitioned
for his opposite. This is the entire hymn:

Ares, superior force,
Ares, chariot rider,
Ares wears gold helmet,
Ares has mighty heart,
Ares, shield-bearer,
Ares, guardian of city,
Ares has armor of bronze,
Ares has powerful arms,
Ares never gets tired,
Ares, hard with spear,
Ares, rampart of Olympos,
Ares, father of Victory
who herself delights in war,
Ares, helper of Justice,
Ares overcomes other side,
Ares leader of most just men,
Ares carries staff of manhood,
Ares turns his fiery bright cycle
among the Seven-signed tracks
of the aether, where flaming chargers
bear him forever
over the third orbit!

Hear me,
helper of mankind,
dispenser of youth's sweet courage,
beam down from up there
your gentle light
on our lives,
and your martial power,
so that I can shake off
cruel cowardice
from my head,
and diminish that deceptive rush
of my spirit, and restrain
that shrill voice in my heart
that provokes me
to enter the chilling din of battle.

Ares is being asked to relieve the petitioner from falling into identification with the god because he does not want to rush wildly into battle. He goes on to say:

You, happy god,
give me courage,
let me linger
in the safe laws of peace,
and thus escape
from battles with enemies
and the fate of a violent death.[7]

It is astonishing that in the eighth century BC Ares should be prayed to as a bringer of peace, but it is archetypally sound. Unless we have relation to the principle, we will fall victim to its negative manifestation. If we are not willing to fight when required, if we cannot summon up aggressive energy when it is appropriate, we will succumb to it in some other way. We will fall victim to someone else's aggression or to our own autonomous assertive energy that can destroy by emerging at an inappropriate time. For example, a patient who possessed that trait repeatedly got into altercations with policemen, instead of applying his aggression to such areas of his life as dealing with his dependency, which might lead to his becoming more effective as a person. He would have done well to pray to Ares to release him, so that he could diminish that "deceptive rush of my spirit and restrain that shrill voice in my heart that provokes me to enter the chilling din of battle."

HEPHAESTUS

Hephaestus, the blacksmith of the gods, was the master of fire and its operations—a metallurgist, a craftsman. He was the son of a single parent, as was Athena, and he was rejected at birth by his mother,

FIG. 9. Hephaestus the artisan presents Thetis with the armor he has made for her son, Achilles. (Detail of an Attic cup, c. 480 BC. Staatliche Museen zu Berlin—Preussicher Kulturbesitz.)

Hera, because of his ugliness and lameness, and was thrown out of heaven, down to earth. A certain analogy exists between the fate of Hephaestus and that of Lucifer, which we can see in Milton's *Paradise Lost*.

Hephaestus is the only god who has a major relation to earth, which became his realm, and he thus signifies the divine power that has descended to earth and has become connected with earthly reality. In him we have a foreshadowing of the Incarnation image, of god becoming human. Hephaestus is a worker in concrete reality, since he is earthbound, and stands for the archetypal factor that operates within the personal and concrete. He is an inventor of useful, cunning, and beautiful devices, and a creative artist.

Hephaestus' companions were Cabiri—the dactyls, the mysterious chthonic dwarf gods who were linked both to creativity and deformity. Hephaestus represents creativity that develops out of defect or out of need; he is the only manifestation of imperfection in this whole Olympian realm of perfect beings. That makes him particularly precious, at least to man, since it gives imperfect man a partner in the divine realm, a partner related to creativity. Psychologically this indicates that an archetypal power has entered into personal reality and has brought the creative principle to the earthly realm. It suggests that creativity is born out of a sense of defectiveness or inadequacy that requires extraordinary effort as a consequence. "Necessity is the mother of invention" is a Hephaestian principle. Although he was married to Aphrodite, she had a love affair with Ares, so Hephaestus is the archetypal cuckold. He might even be considered to stand for the creative aspect of impotence.

The Hephaestian principle, as it has developed, breaks into two streams: on the one hand into the artist and craftsman, the artistic principle emphasizing beauty, and on the other, into the engineer and mechanic, emphasizing utility. For a while at least, the alchemists combined the Hermetic principle and the Hephaestian principle because they were dealing simultaneously with symbolic, philosophic matters, the Hermetic aspect, and, as they labored over their fires, with concrete material, the Hephaestian aspect. This broke apart in the seventeenth century and the Hephaestian aspect went its own way in science and technology. Only now is the Hermetic aspect starting to reemerge in depth psychology, which does not confine itself to the Hermetic principle, but is a new combination of the two. Depth psychology is not just an abstract theoretical doctrine, but a practical operation that has its Hephaestian component in the process of psychotherapy.

The Hephaestian temperament is to be found particularly in artists and craftsmen, in those who live by beauty and those who live by utility—mechanics and makers of all kinds. Such a temperament is preoccupied with work of the hands, with earthy, concrete manifestations: occupational therapy, practical, empirical functioning, and craftsmanship of every sort.

As we look over the masculine side of the Pantheon, setting aside Zeus and his brothers, we can see Apollo, Hermes, Ares, and Hephaestus as four principles of masculine psychological functioning. We can imagine them as they operated in that immense project of the 1960s that sent a man to the moon. It was Apollonian man, represented by the scientists and the planners and their ideas, who made that leap possible, while Hephaestian man, signified by the engineers and the factory workers, made the equipment and the hardware that brought success. Arean man, represented by the astronauts, had the courage and the aggressive energy to make the trip, and Hermetic man, in those who are yet to come, will grasp the larger, hidden, and symbolic meaning of the arrival of man on the moon.

4

The Olympian Goddesses

HERA

FIRST AMONG the female deities on Olympus was Hera, queen of heaven, the wife and equal of Zeus. She was the embodiment of the feminine aspect of the Self, the goddess of wifehood, motherhood, and the rights and power of women.

The myths about Hera that have come down to us focus primarily on her as an outraged spouse. Presumably this reflects the fact that the Greek myths were a product of the masculine psyche, and all the goddesses are seen through that lens. Despite this patriarchal distortion, however, it remains clear that basically as much power and effectiveness adhere to the feminine principle as to the masculine. Zeus has to take Hera into account. Beyond her fury at Zeus' persistent affairs, Hera would also nurse long-term resentments toward certain of the human heroes: for instance Heracles and Aeneas. Yet her harassing and plaguing had the effect of goading these heroes on to greater accomplishment. Although the myth expresses the theme in negative terms, the net result is development.

The picture of marital quarreling between Zeus and Hera, which eventually became a scandal to the more sophisticated Greeks, depicts symbolically the conflict between the masculine and feminine

FIG. 10. Hera with Prometheus. (Detail of an Attic cylix, c. 450 BC. Bibliothèque Nationale, Paris. Photo: Giraudon/Art Resource, New York.)

principles; further, it shows clearly that the masculine principle is not omnipotent; it can be effectively challenged by its opposite, which is represented in the myths by the queenly figure of Hera.

As a type, the Hera woman has a regal, aristocratic, born-to-command quality. She is one who can be a generous patroness, and she always assumes the right to be in charge—the grande dame. To encounter the Hera principle internally means to make contact with the inner feminine as an authority to be served, which, for a woman, would be her core experience. In a man's psychology, Hera can represent the authoritarian aspect of the mother complex, against which the masculine ego must establish itself. In more developed men, meeting Hera would mean experiencing the feminine principle as something to be served as distinct from the masculine logos principle. The Hera principle embodies the idea of the power and the authority of the feminine requiring one's respect and, in some circumstances, worship.

HESTIA

Hestia is the goddess of the sacred hearth, both of the home and of the nation. She drew far more attention in Roman culture than in Greek, the Romans calling her Vesta. She personified the glowing fire on the family hearth, the natural center of the family and of gatherings of family or clan. This domestic hearth was also a sacrificial altar and Hestia was mentioned first and last in every sacrificial ceremony. She signifies the sacredness of being centered, rooted, and contained in a collective group and in a particular region, a local soil. In Rome a great cult was served by Vestal Virgins, who fed an eternal flame honoring sacred loyalty to family, tribe, city, and nation.

The geographical place that nurtures individuals, especially in their first years, tends to remain numinous throughout their lives. This can

FIG. 11. Hestia. (Detail of an Attic cup, c. 520 BC. Museo Nazionale, Tarquinia. Photo: Soprintendenza Archeologica per Etruria Meridionale.)

be seen as the source of patriotism, flag worship, and the nostalgia always attaching to the place one came from, to "home." Hestia represents that. In many analyses that penetrate at all deeply, one encounters some evidence of what could be called the "geographical soul," an aspect of the psyche that has been determined by the geography out of which one was born. Often with the descendants of immigrants, who have only a generation or two of residence in this country, this soul is to be found in the country from which their parents and grandparents came. But also one finds quite recognizable geographical souls of various kinds within the United States—a certain Southern soul, a Midwestern soul, a New England soul. They have been determined by native locality. All of this belongs to the realm of Hestia. It is not possible to worship at the hearth of the human family—that is, the cosmopolitan whole—until one has first worshiped, and still worships, at the hearth of one's more particular locality. For the larger and more comprehensive viewpoint to be authentic, it must be based on a solid relation to one's particular origins; otherwise, cosmopolitanism can be nothing more than alienation.

On a certain building in New Haven, Connecticut, a plaque reads "For God, for country and for Yale." That is an inscription to Hestia in her different manifestations, her different hearths at which one has to serve.

DEMETER

Demeter was the earth mother, the embodiment of agriculture and specifically of grain. An entire myth and cult associated with her grew into the Eleusinian mysteries, which will be considered later. She is the embodiment of the nourishing mother, an archetypal image well known to psychotherapists. In clinical practice, the nourishing mother is a double image. It implies a mother giving nourishment and an infant receiving it, and it is easy for that dynamic to shift so that the nourishing mother becomes a devouring mother, the process of being fed shifting from the infant to the mother. Any woman who

FIG. 12. Demeter, holding a torch and grain stalks, sends Triptolemus forth in a chariot drawn by winged snakes to teach agriculture to mankind. (Detail of an Attic skyphos, c. 480 BC. Copyright British Museum, London.)

is powerfully identified with Demeter and has a compulsive need to nourish, turns into a devouring mother. If she insists on feeding and caretaking, whether it is needed or not, the offspring remains infantile and its potential for growth is injured. The mother who must herself be fed by her children's dependence on her, devours them. This gives rise to the image of the devouring jaws of the negative mother.

ARTEMIS

Artemis, Diana to the Romans, was associated with the moon and was the sister of Apollo, the sun. She was the goddess of the forest and the hunt, an archeress who carried a silver bow. She was virginal and brought health and well-being to virginal maidens, and was the goddess who watched over childbirth; but she was cold, chaste, and

FIG. 13. Artemis threatens Actaeon, who is set upon by
his own dogs. (Attic krater, c. 460 BC. Courtesy Museum of Fine
Arts, Boston. James Fund and by special contribution.)

quick to be offended by men. She was the lady of the beasts, valuing
wild nature more than human feelings and relationships. One of the
classic stories tells of Actaeon's encounter with her in the forest. He
watched her while she was bathing, for which she turned him into a
stag. He was then torn apart by his dogs, an image suggesting that
Actaeon ran afoul of his own instincts. His ego was not up to such a
numinous encounter with deity. It is always a dangerous thing to
stumble over such transpersonal energies unexpectedly, when the ego
is unprepared.

Another side of Artemis' nature is shown in her relationship with
Orion. Her brother, Apollo, was jealous of Artemis' love for Orion,
a great hunter. When Orion was swimming far out in the ocean one
day, Apollo said to Artemis, challenging her competitiveness, "Can
you hit that speck in the ocean with your bow and arrow?" She
aimed with great care and hit it with her arrow, and the speck was
Orion. This pictures how relationships can be destroyed in the Artemis woman through the jealousy of the spiritual animus, here signi-

fied by Apollo. It is as if the woman already has a partner within her own psyche, which wants no competitors from the human realm.

The Artemis woman tends to be efficient, self-sufficient, and not amenable to personal intimacy. As an inner experience, the Artemis principle appears as an attitude that is coldly factual and impersonal and can be as aloof and indifferent as nature. It will be experienced as cruel because it is indifferent to personal human feelings and harsh toward weakness and regressive tendencies. The Artemis woman is devoid of sentimentality in contrast to Demeter, who tends to be sentimental and protective. One might say that Artemis believes in survival of the fittest, and in men we might call her the natural anima. She has no compunctions about being cruel to weakness, but is helpful to strength, and so is growth-promoting to those for whom growth is possible; she will be hated by the regressive side of humanity.

APHRODITE

Aphrodite was the goddess of love and beauty. Her son was Eros, who aroused passion by shooting his victims with arrows. The three Graces are associated with Aphrodite, whose qualities are grace, charm, seductive desire, and the power of the pleasure principle. Despite these attractions, the myths suggest that there are many hazards in her realm. Adonis, her young lover, was killed by a boar one day while he was hunting. In some versions of the myth, this boar was actually Ares, who was also Aphrodite's lover and attacked Adonis out of jealousy. The story suggests that one must be in good relation with the Ares principle of aggression if one is to have an encounter with Aphrodite.

While entanglement with Aphrodite can lead to danger, to scorn her can be disastrous also. We see this in the myth of Hippolytus, who was a devotee of Artemis and so valued chastity above all, refusing the call of love. In retaliation for this slight, Aphrodite cast a spell over his stepmother Phaedra, causing her to fall passionately in love with him. Phaedra made advances to him and then, when he rejected

FIG. 14. Aphrodite and Pan play at dice. (Detail of an incised bronze mirror, c. 375 BC. Copyright British Museum, London.)

her, told her husband, Theseus, that Hippolytus had sexually molested her (it is similar to the biblical story of Joseph and Potiphar's wife). Theseus prayed to Poseidon for revenge and as a punishment, Hippolytus was dragged to death by his horses; a bull sent by the sea god frightened them. As can be seen in this myth, Aphrodite takes her vengeance against anyone who has rejected her by involving him in some questionable or even perverse erotic situation. While it can be perilous to disregard Aphrodite, it can be equally risky to choose her over other goddesses, which is what Paris did. He was given the task of choosing the most beautiful among Aphrodite, Athena, and Hera, and he chose Aphrodite, which led to the Trojan War. All this shows that there is no easy way through the process of psychological development.

There are other issues here, disquieting ones. The gods and the goddesses are often in opposition. As long as the archetypal powers themselves are divided, the ego is cast in a tragic role, being split by the conflict that exists in the divine realm. As long as there is a multiplicity of principles that has not achieved a decisive unity, life is essentially tragic. It is only with the unification symbolized by monotheism and psychologically represented by the Self that there is a chance to overcome this essential tragedy.

Another hazard encountered by a number of women in mythology was brought about by equating their beauty with Aphrodite's. Some dreadful fate always befell such women for their *hybris*—their consuming pride. This has the clear psychological meaning that beauty and its capacity to engender desire must not be identified with but must be recognized as a divine dynamism. To presume that it belongs to oneself is to identify with Aprodite or to challenge her divine principality. On the other hand, a more appealing aspect of Aphrodite's power is revealed in the myth of Pygmalion. He was a sculptor who fell in love with his ivory statue of a woman and prayed to Aphrodite to bring the statue to life. She granted him his prayer, turning ivory into flesh, indicating that Aphrodite is also a life-producing principle. This story is a beautiful representation of what can happen to the imagery of the inner world if one pours enough energy into it: with the help of Aphrodite it can come to life.

At times Aphrodite is conceived as the basic cosmogonic principle, the very source of life itself. This attitude is illustrated by the opening lines of Lucretius' poem *Of the Nature of Things*. He dedicates his whole poem to Aphrodite—or Venus, as the Romans knew her—and invokes her in these lines:

> Mother of Rome, delight of Gods and men,
> Dear Venus that beneath the gliding stars
> Makest to teem the many-voyaged main
> And fruitful lands—for all of living things
> Through thee alone are evermore conceived,

Through thee are risen to visit the great sun—
Before thee, Goddess, and thy coming on,
Flee stormy wind and massy cloud away,
For thee the daedal Earth bears scented flowers,
For thee the waters of the unvexed deep
Smile, and the hollows of the serene sky
Glow with diffused radiance for thee!
For soon as comes the springtime face of day,
And procreant gales blow from the West unbarred,
First fowls of air, smit to the heart by thee,
Foretoken thy approach, O thou Divine,
And leap the wild herds round the happy fields
Or swim the bounding torrents. Thus amain,
Seized with the spell, all creatures follow thee
Whithersoever thou walkest forth to lead,
And thence through seas and mountains and swift streams,
Through leafy homes of birds and greening plains,
Kindling the lure of love in every breast,
Thou bringest the eternal generations forth,
Kind after kind. And since 'tis thou alone
Guidest the Cosmos, and without thee naught
Is risen to reach the shining shores of light,
Nor aught of joyful or of lovely born,
Thee do I crave co-partner in that verse
Which I presume on Nature to compose. . . .[1]

When we read these lines, we see that the symbolism of Aphrodite overlaps with that of the Holy Ghost, even though one might imagine them to be quite separate. They share, for instance, the symbol of the dove, and as Jung has demonstrated in his *Mysterium Coniunctionis*, especially in the symbolism of what the alchemists called "blessed greenness," we encounter Aphrodite and her life-giving capacities on the one hand, and on the other, the spiritually conceiving power of the Holy Ghost, which was thought of as the color green and can be equated with the vegetation spirit belonging to the life principle of Aphrodite.

One should also note the lines about Aphrodite from Euripides' drama *Hippolytus*; they tell us how the ancients regarded Aphrodite:

> Though the loved Queen's onset in her might is more than men can bear, yet does she gently visit yielding hearts, and only when she finds a proud, unnatural spirit doth she take and mock it past belief. Her path is in the sky, and mid the ocean's surge she rides; from her all nature springs; she sows the seeds of love, inspires the warm desire to which we sons of earth all owe our being.[2]

The Aphrodite woman of the present is a well-known type. She functions through the qualities of charm, appeal, and the ability and willingness to give pleasure and to convey subtle, flattering attention. Of course, as with all the other principles, the individual can fall victim to the Aphrodite function. If she identifies with it, it is as though the archetypal function lives through her and she becomes its helpless servant. We can say that just as the independent Artemis woman could be balanced by some measure of Aphrodite's warmth, so some relation to Artemis would lead the Aphrodite woman to greater self-sufficiency.

The subjective or inner component of Aphrodite can be seen in an introverted or an extraverted way. Internally, it could mean the ability to relate to the beautiful, since beauty is an important characteristic of the Aphrodite function. Externally it would encompass the whole principle of Eros, the willingness to connect with and to be considerate of the other. This ability to make a life-enhancing connection with another is linked with Aphrodite's whole capacity for engendering and enlarging life.

ATHENA

Athena was the chief deity of Athens, and a huge statue of her stood in the Parthenon. We might say that Athena stands as the goddess of Western civilization, since it originated in her city. She was born out of the forehead of Zeus, without a mother. According to the story,

FIG. 15. Athena with spear and shield bearing the image of Medusa. (Detail of an Attic amphora, c. 480 BC. Antikenmuseum Basel und Sammlung Ludwig.)

Zeus swallowed her mother, Metis, before Athena's birth and then brought her forth himself through the forehead. Like Hephaestus, she is a one-parent figure; in her case this signifies a feminine content that is oriented toward the masculine and particularly helpful to it.

She is the principle that brings about civilization. She was thought of as introducing the plow and the olive tree, which were looked upon as the origins of civilized life. She appeared helmeted and was considered a warrior goddess, but in terms of strategy rather than of violence. She was a bringer of practical knowledge, and as her image developed, it took on more and more the explicit qualities of wisdom. She was a protector of heroes and brought wise counsel and victory to them. The outstanding example was Perseus, to whom she supplied the mirror shield that is discussed below. She has many parallels to the Jewish wisdom figure, not the least of which is the fact that she was Zeus' favorite child. The parallel is exemplified in a few verses from the Biblical book of Proverbs in which the feminine personification of wisdom speaks of herself as Yahweh's favorite child. In the eighth chapter of Proverbs we read:

The Lord created me the beginning of his works,
before all else that he made, long ago.
Alone, I was fashioned in times long past,
at the beginning, long before earth itself.
When there was yet no ocean I was born,
no springs brimming with water.
Before the mountains were settled in their place,
long before the hills I was born
when as yet he had made neither land nor lake
nor the first clod of earth.
When he set the heavens in their place I was there,
when he girdled the ocean with the horizon,
when he fixed the canopy of clouds overhead
and set the springs of ocean firm in their place,
when he prescribed its limits for the sea
and knit together earth's foundations.
Then I was at his side each day,
his darling and delight,
playing in his presence continually,
playing on the earth, when he had finished it,
while my delight was in mankind.[3]

Linked images such as these of Athena and the Biblical wisdom figure demonstrate how the same archetypal reality springs up in different cultures and reveals its essential similarity, since it corresponds to a basic inner experience of mankind.

Psychologically, the Athena woman is a familiar figure, one who puts primary emphasis on spirit and intelligence, who is a companion and advisor to men, often without erotic involvement. In her past history one generally finds a positive relation to the father and a questionable relation with the mother—in other words, she is the creature of one parent. She is apt to be a woman who is particularly skilled at building bridges for the man between his mind and his feeling. She meets him more than halfway, and hence she is especially valuable as an intellectual and spiritual companion. Taken as an inner principle, an aspect of a man's psyche, she is a most significant figure. Jung identifies the feminine figure of wisdom, Sophia, as the highest manifestation of the anima, the inner spiritual guide, even more developed than the purely spiritual image of the heavenly Mary. It is an image of woman that can relate a man to his depths in a profound and comprehensive way.

As a final observation, it may be noted that Greek philosophers were lovers of Sophia, as the word "philosophy" indicates, and Athena was closely connected with her. Hence, it is quite appropriate that Western philosophy should have had its birth in Athena's city.

5

The Heroes

HERACLES

WHAT DOES the hero figure mean psychologically? The hero can be thought of as a dynamism toward a certain kind of psychological achievement or service, more concretely as a personification of the urge to individuation. The hero is linked both to the Self and to the ego but is neither one of them. The heroic urge, the urge to individuation, is an expression of the Self, the greater personality, but the conscious ego must relate to this urge and act on it in order to make it a reality. We could say, then, that the hero is more than the ego and less than the Self. It is important that the ego should not identify itself with the hero figure, although there is a widespread tendency in youth to do just that and to overestimate the ego's power.

In considering this interpretation of the hero figure, it will be helpful to recall Jung's definition of the term individuation. He says this:

> In general, it is the process by which individual beings are formed and differentiated; in particular, it is the development of the psychological *individual* as a being distinct from the general, collective psychology. Individuation, therefore, is a process of *differentiation,* having for its goal the development of the individual personality.[1]

In another place he defines the individual as

> . . . characterized by a peculiar, and in some respects unique psychology. The peculiar character of the individual psyche appears less in its

elements than in its complex formations. The psychological individual
. . . has an *a priori* unconscious existence, but exists consciously only
in so far as a consciousness of his peculiar nature is present, i.e., so far
as there exists a conscious distinction from other individuals.[2]

By this definition individuation and the growth of consciousness are
really the same thing. Individuals are the only carriers of consciousness, which means that there is no such thing as "collective consciousness," since, to the extent that a given psychic content is
collective, it is not related to and carried by the individual, and hence
is not really conscious. The myths about the hero figure depict a
striving toward the realization of individual uniqueness, that is,
toward becoming a carrier of more and more consciousness.

It is only proper to start with Heracles (more familiarly the Roman
Hercules) since he is the hero of heroes in Western culture, his name
almost synonymous with the hero function. Heracles and his twin,
Iphicles, were the sons of the mortal woman Alcmene. Iphicles was
fathered by Alcmene's husband, Amphitryon, and Heracles was fathered by Zeus, who came to Alcmene in Amphitryon's form. It is as
though we have the image of ego represented by Iphicles, and the
heroic function represented by Heracles, the difference between them
becoming immediately apparent. Shortly after Heracles' birth, Hera
sent two poisonous serpents to the cradle of the twins. Iphicles
shrieked in terror, but Heracles grabbed the two serpents by the neck
and strangled them, depicting the difference in reactivity between the
human ego and the heroic principle.

Heracles' name means glory either by, through, or of Hera.
Throughout his life Heracles was plagued by Hera—she was his
enemy—yet his name indicates that his glory is somehow related to
his connection with her, and in fact something about the harassment
itself served to promote his achievement. This is reminiscent of Job
being plagued by Yahweh, and suggests a divided state within the
divine realm: one aspect of the divine nourishes and supports and the
other aspect challenges and goads. In Job's case, at the same time
that he was suffering the results of Yahweh's wager with Satan, he
retained his trust in the redeeming aspect of Yahweh.

The features of the birth of Heracles exemplify the birth of the hero in general. This was first elucidated by Otto Rank in his book *The Myth of the Birth of the Hero,* which points out a number of common characteristics that can be seen also in the lives of two other heroes, Moses and Jesus.[3] First, the hero almost always has a double parentage. Heracles' double fathers were Amphitryon and Zeus. Moses had his own parents but was adopted by the princess of the royal household and raised by royalty, while Jesus, in addition to Joseph and Mary, had a suprapersonal parent in the Holy Spirit. A second typical event of the hero's story is that immediately after birth he is abandoned or else subject to severe attacks or threats. Heracles' life was put in danger by the two serpents sent by Hera; Moses experienced abandonment; and Jesus was threatened by the Massacre of the Innocents. A third common theme is that shortly after his appearance the hero child demonstrates miraculous or almost invincible powers, Heracles' strangling of the snakes providing an example. In Louis Ginsberg's *Legends of the Bible* we find the story that at Moses' birth a radiance emanated from him and that he walked and spoke on his first day.[4] Similarly, Apocryphal stories tell us that on the holy family's way to Egypt miracles took place—wheat fields sprang up in one day and heathen idols broke and tumbled with the passage of the infant Jesus.

These instances reflect a theme that comes up not infrequently in dreams at important periods of transition: the birth of the wonder child. In psychological terms, the double parentage motif tells us that the urge to individuation has a twofold source: personal factors and also transpersonal ones. It stems from the care and loving attention that actual persons such as the parents give the individual, but it derives as well from the archetypal roots of its own being, from divine knowledge.

The miraculous powers of the divine child symbolize the power of the urge toward individuation. The child has contact with a source of extraordinary potency. At the same time, the hero child is exposed to great threat, symbolized by the dangers it encounters. When the potentiality for individuation is first being born, everything is against it. It is perfectly understandable that this special urge to develop into a unique being, different from all others and from conventional standards, cannot expect to find outer support. Others may simply have no interest in the new being, or, more commonly, the environment and conventionalities of all kinds oppose it, perhaps quite subtly. It may be opposed by being regarded as worthless. That can be a killing danger, of course, because something that is newly born requires attention and nourishment and is extremely vulnerable to indifference.

Heracles had a tempestuous youth. He was subject to fits of anger and in one such fury, with his great strength, he killed Linus, the music instructor, and was banished to the country as a shepherd. This was only the first of several states of violent possession that had important consequences. The image expresses the fact that individuation energy is dangerous when the conscious ego is still weak and undisciplined. Jung told the story about himself that as a child he was subject to bouts of rage that frightened him. On one occasion, when he had been waylaid by a gang of local peasant boys, he became possessed by rage and seized one of the boys by the feet and used him as a club to beat off the others. He was amazed by the strength that welled up in him, realizing that in such a state he could have killed someone. This possession is quite analogous to Heracles', and indicative of what can happen to someone with an exceptional energy potential.

The majority of us cannot call upon that excess of energy, so we are easily tamed by conventional means. But a few people of the Heraclean type, falling victim to their surplus of individuation energy, must undergo Heraclean tasks of differentiation and transformation of that energy. The most significant feature of the Heracles myth began in such a fit of rage, in a state of madness sent by Hera, when Heracles killed his wife and children. It is surprising, of course, that a hero myth of ancient times would include such human fallibility in the supreme hero, but it is authentic psychologically, because it is just such an event that can engender the most profound effort at transformation of the raw energy. In his state of remorse and despair Heracles consulted the Delphic oracle on how to redeem himself and be purified. Receiving no response, Heracles then tried to steal the tripod of the oracle in order to set up one of his own to get an answer.

He actually wrestled with Apollo for the tripod, an act reminiscent of Jacob's wrestling with the angel or Menelaus' wrestling with Proteus in order to extract some message, some understanding. The point is that Heracles was so insistent on knowing what he must do to be redeemed that Zeus eventually intervened, and he was told by the oracle that he must turn himself over as a slave to Eurystheus, his cousin. In order to work out his criminal behavior he must perform twelve labors.

This leads us into the image of the servant hero, of which Heracles is probably the first and best example. We have later expressions of this—almost all heroes perform tasks—but the service, indeed the state of slavery, that is specified in the Heracles myth is unique. It anticipates a later version of the same theme in Isaiah, which describes the suffering servant of Yahweh, and there is also a connection with the Biblical statement that "he who is first among you, let him be servant of all." Heracles is an original example of the psychological truth that the finest aspect of the psyche serves by its very nature; it gives, rather than receives.

Heracles is obliged to perform labors, to undertake a great work, in somewhat the same sense that the alchemist undertook his task of the transformation of matter. Heracles' question to the oracle, of how one can be purified after a violent possession, can be answered psychologically as "become a slave to the work of individuation." This great opus of individuation is described symbolically in the twelve labors of Heracles.

We can consider the labors to represent a series of encounters with the unconscious in its different aspects, and they are quite pertinent images to meditate on. The first task was to kill and flay the Nemean lion, which was ravaging the country. The lion is an image expressive of belligerent, masculine, instinctual energy. So Heracles' initial task was to come to grips with the very energy that caused him to become a criminal in the first place. Not only did he have to kill the lion, he had to flay it, to skin it. But the hide of this beast was so tough it was impervious to all blades; nothing would cut it. Heracles managed to kill the lion by strangling it and then flayed it with its own claws. This is an early reference to a theme repeated in alchemy advising

FIG. 16. Heracles, wearing the skin of the
Nemean lion, steals the Delphic tripod. (De-
tail of an Attic amphora, c. 480 BC. Martin von
Wagner Museum, University of Würzburg.
Photo: K. Oehrlein.)

that a substance be dissolved in its own water, or calcined in its own
fire. Such a prescription is nonsensical by all ordinary criteria, but
psychologically we know that it refers to the fact that a complex, the
psychic content that one has to deal with, contains its own potentiality for transformation if one can locate and relate to it; only by using
its own energies can the work be done, since the ego does not have
the necessary power. So it was with the Nemean lion—it could be
flayed only by its own claws. Heracles clothed himself with the skin
and wore it ever afterward, with the jaws of the lion sticking up over
his head; it became a kind of cloak of invulnerability similar to a
dream image in which one is wearing a fur coat; the lion's skin is

Heracles' fur coat. He has mastered or come to terms with a certain primordial instinctual energy, and now it no longer threatens to overwhelm him. Now it protects him and belongs to him. We could say that this formerly wild aggressive energy is now in the service of the ego.

This passage from Nietzsche's essay "Homer's Contest" illustrates what the lion might have symbolized and what Heracles' task would have signified for the Greeks:

[The Greeks have a trait of cruelty that really must strike fear into our hearts.] When the victor in a fight among the cities executes the entire male citizenry in accordance with the laws of war, and sells all the women and children into slavery, we see in the sanction of such a law that the Greeks considered it an earnest necessity to let their hatred flow forth fully; in such moments crowded and swollen feeling relieved itself: the tiger [read lion] leaped out, voluptuous cruelty in his terrible eyes. Why must the Greek sculptor give forth again and again to war and combat in innumerable repetitions: distended human bodies, their sinews tense with hatred or with the arrogance of triumph; writhing bodies, wounded; dying bodies, expiring? Why did the whole Greek world exult over the combat scenes of *The Iliad?*[5]

This cruelty is the Nemean lion that Heracles has to conquer; this is what the lion referred to for the ancient Greeks, and although we no longer have a Nemean lion today, we are not so remote from what it stands for.

After this first and all the subsequent labors, Eurystheus, the man who gave Heracles his orders, was terrified by the sight of the hero returning in triumph after overcoming these great monsters. Heracles had taken into himself the power of the creature he had overcome, and Eurystheus could not face him directly. He would only meet Heracles protected by a great urn, a scene represented on a good many Greek vases: Eurystheus peeking out of a huge urn as Heracles returns with one of his trophies. Eurystheus' fear corresponds to that of the ego, which stands in awe of the heroic energy, and is well advised to be afraid of it; if it is not, it may identify with it.

Heracles' second labor was to overcome the hydra of Lerna, a monster with poisonous breath that would generate two heads any time one was cut off. This is an apt image of a certain aspect of the unconscious that cannot be dealt with by ordinary means. One sees it represented in dreams in which the dreamer, encountering some small creature, perhaps an insect or reptile, tries furiously to stamp it to death, only to watch it grow bigger. The hydra has something of that same nature: one head is cut off and two emerge. Some new method had to be devised to deal with the hydra, so Heracles persuaded his nephew Iolaus to assist him, and as soon as one head was cut off, Iolaus immediately cauterized it, which prevented it from regrowing. This seems to refer to the application of affect: not only is there a discriminating operation, signified by the clean cut of the blade, but there is also an application of affective intensity—fire—that produces the cauterizing effect.

The problem of the hydra is probably related to repression, since another of its attributes was that one of its heads was immortal; even when it was cut off it remained invulnerable and it had to be buried under a big rock, a repressive operation. We can say that Heracles dealt with the hydra of Lerna by repressive measures, a stratagem that led in the long run to his undoing. After he had disposed of the hydra, he took its poison and used it thereafter to tip his arrows. As we shall see, the poison of the hydra finally destroyed Heracles himself.

The third labor required capturing the Ceryneian hind, a female deer sacred to Artemis, which nevertheless had brazen hooves and golden horns. The image of this deer suggests that a masculine value (the golden horns) was being carried by a feminine principle. The Artemis principle had to be encountered, then tamed and brought back as a part of masculine consciousness.

As his fourth labor Heracles had to capture the Erymanthian boar, the creature that killed Adonis and also Attis, the son and lover of the Great Mother Cybele. The boar can be thought of as the crude phallic power of the Great Mother that is still under control of the matriarchal psyche. To overcome the Erymanthian boar would involve the hero's coming into contact with a certain aspect of primordial feminine power and mastering it.

Cleaning the Augean stables came next on Heracles' agenda and was accomplished by diverting a river through them. They had accumulated vast quantities of manure, an image that has parallels in dreams of overflowing toilets with feces spilling out, and of long-neglected outhouses. Those are modern, individual versions of the Augean stables, indicating long neglect of the instinctive processes, and requiring Heraclean effort in attending to them and giving them their due.

The sixth task was to dispose of the Stymphalian birds, huge creatures with brazen beaks and feathers and poisonous excrement who lived in a swamp that was neither land nor water. They were scattered by the use of noisemakers like rattles and we can think of them as evil spirits, negative autonomous complexes that were exorcised by raising a counterspirit against them. The image of the Stymphalian birds and the way Heracles dealt with them might come to mind when one encounters people who, unable to stand normal silence, chatter perpetually. Perhaps they are compelled to make noise in order to frighten their Stymphalian birds away.

The hero's seventh labor, the capture of the Cretan bull that was ravaging the island, involves symbolism taken up again in the myth of Theseus. The bull, along with the lion, represents an aspect of masculine, instinctual energy and is one of the manifestations of Zeus, who carried away Europa as a bull. It has a lengthy symbolism. The basic image of Mithraism was the sacrifice of the bull, and the bullfight ritual that still exists in Spanish cultures belongs to this same symbolism. In dreams the bull generally expresses the dangerous chthonic aspect of masculine power, the quality that Heracles is obliged to encounter and deal with. An example of this was a patient's dream following a psychotic episode: the dream consisted of the simple statement, "The bull is loose."

The next episode concerns the man-eating mares of Diomedes, who would feed his guests to them. The imagery here refers to coming to grips with the devouring aspects of the unconscious, which is not always hospitable.

The ninth labor is a little different. The hero was required to fetch the golden girdle of Ares worn by Hippolyte, the queen of the Amazons, a race of warlike females. The word amazon means "without breasts," and the story relates that these women would amputate the right breast in order to be better archers. At the same time, to be born male in the world of the Amazons was a disaster, because a male child's leg was broken at birth to ensure that it would grow up crippled. Here we have a picture of the matriarchal psyche, and to take the girdle of Ares from the queen of the Amazons meant redeeming the masculine principle, which was under subjection to the matriarchal aspect of the psyche.

The account of the tenth labor, the return of the cattle of the giant Geryon, who was located somewhere at the limits of the known world, takes us on a long, meandering journey in which Heracles travels all the way out beyond the Rock of Gibraltar and back, his main activity consisting of civilizing whatever he comes to. He tames wild beasts, founds cities, and colonizes various places he passes through—this is a portrait of Heracles as a culture hero civilizing the barbarians, foreshadowing what the Greeks in fact would eventually carry out in the Mediterranean basin.

As his penultimate task Heracles was to fetch the golden apples in the garden of the Hesperides, which were protected by a dragon that lay coiled around the tree—a setting, of course, reminiscent of the Garden of Eden. Heracles had to call upon the Titan Atlas to locate the garden and agreed to hold up the world while Atlas plucked the golden apples for him. Atlas saw a chance to get rid of his heavy burden, and would have left Heracles holding the world, but Heracles tricked him into reassuming the burden by asking him to take it back for just a minute while he placed a pad on his shoulder.

There is something analogous here to the story of Saint Christopher, the giant ferryman who carried across a stream an infant who got heavier and heavier until finally he was struggling under the weight of the whole world, after which he learned he had been bearing the infant Jesus. Here we have a similar idea. It tells us that the apples of the Hesperides and the whole image of paradise are expressions of wholeness, which cannot be reached unless one can carry the weight of wholeness, the weight of the world, on one's shoulders. This is not a permanent task—it should not be that—but it has to be

taken on for a moment. Then there is the problem of getting it off
again.

On Heracles' return with the golden apples, he met the giant Alcy-
oneus, who forced him into a wrestling match. The giant was constantly rejuvenated by contact with the earth, so that every time in
the wrestling match that he suffered a fall, he was reinvigorated.
Things went badly for Heracles until he realized what to do; he killed
the giant while holding him aloft and not allowing him to touch the
earth. Here again is the image of bearing a weight rather than letting
it fall, which corresponds psychologically to what is required at a
certain point in coming to terms with an unconscious complex. Such
a pocket of energy and affect from the unconscious, which tends to
take the ego by surprise and trigger an emotional outburst, must be
held in awareness until it has exhausted its quantity of unconscious
energy, until it has "cooled off." If it is let go too soon, it is reinforced
by its contact with the depths.

At last Heracles ended his servitude with the capture of Cerberus,
the dog of hell. This seems to be the negative version of a previous
task. The paradisal garden of the Hesperides represents the positive
aspect of contact with the center, the Self, but here we have a descent
into hell instead of an ascent into paradise. Heracles brought Cerberus up to earth, exposing him to consciousness, so that the horror
of the dark side of the Self was seen and could no longer be doubted.
By contrast, the apples of the Hesperides were a powerful token of
the beatific aspect of the Self.

There is another episode in which Heracles, thinking he had been
accused of stealing cattle by an old man named Iphitus, murdered
him in a fit of rage. To redeem himself for that crime he became a
slave of Omphale, an Anatolian queen, who dressed him in skirts and
made him weave and amuse her. He succumbed totally to feminine
domination. Once again we come upon a theme that is almost un-
heard of in a hero myth, but its true-to-life quality is striking. It implies that after living out of and serving the masculine principle so
extremely, the hero must submit himself to the service of the feminine, a notion that we see again in medieval chivalry, where the
knight would commit himself to the service of his mistress. It indi-

cates the extent to which the male ego is obliged to strip itself of its masculine identity in the course of the individuation process.

Heracles is associated with various other feats, and one other important episode brings the hydra back into the picture. The story has it that Heracles wanted to marry Deianeira, but in order to do so he had to wrestle with Achelous, the river god, who also sought her hand. Achelous was a strange creature who could take three different forms: that of a bull, a speckled serpent, and a bull-headed man—not unlike Proteus, who was able to transform himself almost indefinitely. This is the theme of the monster that must be overcome in order to rescue the anima, and it tells us that the relationship function in a man has to be won; it is not given automatically but has to be carved out of the whole area of unregenerate concupiscence that he starts out with. This primitive desirousness is symbolized by Achelous, the river god.

Heracles overcame Achelous and won Deianeira as his wife. But at a river crossing, the centaur Nessus, who had offered to take Deianeira across the stream, attempted to rape her in the middle of the crossing. Heracles immediately responded by killing him with one of his arrows tipped in the poisonous gall of the hydra. As Nessus was dying, he said to Deianeira, "Take some of my blood. It is a love charm and if ever you're in danger of losing the love of Heracles to another, you can apply this charm and it will regain his love for you." What he gave her was his blood containing the hydra poison. Later, when Heracles became enamored of another, Iole, Deianeira made use of what Nessus had given her. She dipped a shirt in the poisoned blood and sent it to Heracles, thinking she would thereby win him back. But as Heracles put on the shirt it burst into flame and he could not tear it off. His only release was to lie down and be consumed by the flames of his own funeral pyre, at which point he ascended to heaven and joined the gods as a divinity.

There are some weighty implications in this symbolism. Many analogies to the crucifixion and ascension of Christ are present, and the story is worked out by means of naive images that tell us much about the primitive psyche and the nature of desirousness. The poison of the hydra, which had for so long made Heracles invincible, finally destroyed him. As we noticed previously, his victory over the hydra had been only partial; it seemed to smack of repression rather than of any decisive transformation. The Nessus episode suggests that the poison that cannot be permanently destroyed and finally turns against the hero can be thought of as primitive desirousness. This is what used to be called concupiscence, which seems to be at the very root of all organic life; it does not differ from original sin. The effect of the hydra poison takes place in the context of desirousness, of lust—the attempted rape by Nessus, the later desire of Heracles for a new mistress, and then the possessive desire of Deianeira. The myth is a dramatization of how this concupiscence, this primordial desirousness, finally burns everything that pertains to it, and the culmination only occurs when another fire, the funeral pyre, overwhelms the flames of desire. It represents a kind of ultimate purification in which a fiery purging of everything that is mortal in Heracles takes place—a final sublimation that transforms him to the eternal state. Although many of Heracles' labors actually symbolize overcoming primitive desirousness, in the end he succumbed to all that he had been struggling against. Yet at the same time his failure was his final victory.

JASON AND MEDEA

The story of Jason and the quest of the golden fleece is a second widely familiar individuation myth of the ancient Greek canon. It was a favorite of the alchemists for whom the golden fleece seemed identical with their own objective of making the incorruptible substance symbolized by gold. They considered Jason an early alchemist.

The tale begins long before Jason's birth. There had been a crime that was to have led to the sacrifice of two children, Helle and Phrixus, but they were able to escape owing to the miraculous appearance of a ram with golden fleece (this calls to mind Isaac's deliverance from Abraham's effort to sacrifice him by the appearance of a ram in a thicket). The ram with the golden fleece carried the children from Greece to Colchis, on the far side of the Black Sea. Helle was lost when she fell into the Hellespont, which took her name, but Phrixus survived and became an exile in Colchis, where the ram was sacrificed and the golden fleece was hung up as a shrine.

The ram with the golden fleece signifies a masculine aspect of the Self. Its golden fleece suggests its supreme value, but its masculine character indicates that it is only a partial expression of the Self, and that limitation runs through the entire myth: much is accomplished, but incompletely. We recognize this theme from the very beginning in the one-sided nature of the symbol and in the early loss of the girl child Helle. The feminine element is lost repeatedly and then at the end, in retaliation, destroys the whole enterprise.

The situation that led up to the expedition is equally instructive psychologically. The initial crime committed in the past, the effects of which had impoverished the country, had to be expiated. This is a version of the theme of original sin that appears in both the Greek and Hebrew traditions: in some early psychological period a sin was committed that now needs restitution. In psychological terms, this refers to some crime against the natural state of things that is necessary for the ego to initiate its own development. An act of violence against the original state is the basis on which the ego evolves and takes for itself energies belonging to nature, but that also has the effect of alienating the ego from the natural condition. In the Jason myth, a kind of sickness lies upon the land because of a missing vital value; the land has been separated from its central meaning, and sooner or later the fruits of that crime come to the fore and must be dealt with. This was Jason's task.

The account of the Argonauts opens at the time when the land was in distress and Jason was a young man, just starting out in life. When Jason was a child, his life had been in danger and he had been smuggled out of the royal palace to be raised by Cheiron, the centaur. When he was fully grown, he returned home to confront his uncle Pelias, who had usurped the kingdom. An oracle had warned Pelias to beware a man with one sandal, and the story relates that as Jason was heading for the city, intending to demand the throne as his rightful inheritance, he offered an old crone assistance in crossing a river. (Crucial events, often mishaps, tend to happen at rivers, as Jung has noted; it is the theme of the dangerous transition.) As he carried her across the river, the woman grew ever heavier and it turned out that she was Hera herself. Barely making it across, Jason lost one of his sandals, and here again is the Saint Christopher reference: it is as if the hero, as he proceeds to meet his destiny, encounters a certain aspect of the unconscious that leaves its mark on him. A variation on the theme of laming, Jason's lost sandal corresponds, for example, to Captain Ahab's wooden leg in *Moby-Dick* and to Oedipus' damaged foot.

When Jason arrived in the city and demanded the return of his throne, Pelias agreed to do so if Jason would bring back the golden fleece and with it the spirit of Phrixus. The oracle had pronounced that the land would not prosper until this was done. Jason thereupon set forth on the voyage of the Argonauts, the most remarkable assemblage of heroes ever brought together for such an adventure.

The first stop of the voyage was the island of Lemnos, where the Argonauts found that the Lemnian women had been insulted by their husbands and in revenge had slaughtered them all. Jason and his group were accordingly welcomed to the beds of the Lemnian women for the sake of the children they could father, and the problem was to get the men back on the ships and on their way again. It is as if, on such a trip to the unconscious, when there is a first reconciliation of opposing factors, a strong temptation arises to succumb to the pleasure urge, to settle for that, and to forget about the goal that is still far distant.

Back on the ships, the crew then suffered the loss of Jason's armor-bearer, Hylas. A beautiful young man, he was drawing water from a spring on another isle when a nymph of the spring fell in love with him and drew him into the water, where he drowned. This suggests a Narcissus-like form of immature romanticism that falls into the unconscious; the implication is that certain qualities cannot survive the journey into the unconscious, but sink into it and perish.

The Argonauts then met an arrogant brute named Amycus, who required that everyone who passed by fight him or be thrown into the sea. Polydeuces accepted his challenge and vanquished him, which we can see as an encounter with arrogant attitudes that must be overcome if the journey into the unconscious is to proceed further.

Next, the crew came upon Phineus and the Harpies. Phineus had a gift for prophecy, but he told too much about the future and Zeus punished him by sending the Harpies, nasty birds who would snatch his food whenever it was laid out and leave a repulsive stench. The Argonauts, however, needed to get directions from Phineus to continue their voyage, and Phineus insisted on being freed from his plague of Harpies before he would give them. This seems to be a picture of contaminated intuition. Intuitive knowledge is necessary if the Argonauts are to proceed, yet it must be purified before it becomes serviceable. One does encounter occasions of misused intuition, which is really not available for conscious purposes but is something the individual falls victim to; it is more a plague than a benefit. Those with a certain kind of extraverted intuition, for instance, can sense what is expected of them by others and then are obliged to serve that expectation, not as a matter of choice but as a compulsion. After Phineus was relieved of the Harpies, he told them the course to follow and how to get through the Symplegades. These were two rocks that crashed together repeatedly; the boat had to slip between them. It is an image of the opposites: one must move between the opposites to go on, but with the risk of getting caught in their clashing.

Eventually, the Argonauts arrived at Colchis where King Aeëtes proved willing to turn over the fleece, providing certain seemingly impossible tasks were performed: two fire-eating brazen bulls must be yoked, a field must be plowed with them, then sown with dragons' teeth, and the armed men that sprang from that sowing must be killed. What seems to be indicated by all of this is that the ego must expose itself to the primordial powers of the masculine archetype represented by the fire-breathing bulls, and the opposites that arise in the form of armed men must also be dealt with. In the event, when the soldiers sprang up, a stone was thrown in their midst and they turned against and annihilated each other. The psychological implication of that image is that one must not identify with one of a pair of warring opposites. If, in one's own psychic conflicts, one can refrain from such an identification, the opposites wear themselves out, leading to a transformation.

None of the tasks could have been carried out, however, without the help of Medea, the king's daughter, who fell in love with Jason at her first sight of the hero. Medea was a sorceress and when Jason promised to take her home in the ship as his wife, she gave him a magic ointment that made him invulnerable for a day and thus enabled him to perform the necessary feats. This help from the anima, who had contact with arcane powers—we could say, with deep layers of the unconscious—was indispensable to his success. She continued to help him when later, King Aeëtes went back on his word to give up the fleece and Jason had to steal it and flee Colchis, followed by the king's ships. From on board the Argo, Medea delayed the pursuing forces by killing her brother Apsyrtus and cutting up his body, throwing one piece after another from the ship. As the father paused to pick up each one, the Argonauts were able to escape.

We are dealing with a version of the widespread theme of dismemberment; here, it is carried out in the service of the hero's task—to get away, get back to consciousness. There are different ways of interpreting this theme, but essentially in this myth Medea's relationship to her brother was sacrificed in the interests of her relationship to Jason. Although the image is repulsive, it represents the dissolving of a certain concretization of libido so that it may become available for a new kind of relationship.

Once the pair returned to Greece, Medea performed yet another service for Jason. Pelias, the usurper, had killed Jason's parents and vengeance was due. Medea tricked Pelias' daughters into killing their aging father by cutting him up, on the assurance that he would be put into a pot and Medea, the sorceress, would magically rejuvenate him. Thus Pelias was dismembered just as Medea's brother had been, and both times the responsibility for these actions was left in the hands of Medea, as Jason's anima. Jason, the masculine ego, avoided responsibility, a fatal mistake on the path to individuation, and a suggestion that there was trouble ahead.

Finally, for reasons of expediency, Jason decided to leave Medea and marry the princess of Thebes (a return of the Deianeira-Heracles

FIG. 17. Medea escapes in a dragon-drawn chariot, while her dead children lie on an altar and Jason looks up after his departing wife. (The Medea krater. Earthenware with slip decoration and added red, white, and yellow, h. 50.3 cm. Attributed to the Policoro Painter, South Italy, late 5th–early 4th century BC. Copyright Cleveland Museum of Art, Leonard C. Hanna, Jr., Fund, 91.1.)

theme). Medea sent a magic robe to the princess, which burst into flames and destroyed her when she put it on. Medea then killed her own children in revenge against Jason and finally disappeared in a dragon chariot into the sky. This was the end of Medea, as far as Jason was concerned. The whole process, the whole Argonaut journey, had failed, essentially because of the disregard of the feminine element. That was presaged at the beginning, when the child, Helle, drowned, and it continued in Jason's use of Medea's powers without honoring his promises to her. Psychologically speaking, a central feature of this myth is the consequence of misusing the anima, the man's feminine side and soul. As with Medea, the anima used to advance the aims of the masculine ego and not granted respect for her own reality, turns bitter and is lost to the man. Ultimately, Jason is said to have lost the favor of the gods and to have become a homeless wanderer.

The story of Jason and Medea seems to live itself out continuously. A man will meet a woman who captures his anima projection and through that projection he will temporarily get a sense of worth and competence and masculine power that carries him on in the life process. But then, since the energy came out of the projection and was not really his own achievement, the time of reckoning will come when the projection fails and he will be left as Jason was with regard to Medea. The job of psychic integration is still to be done. We see this phenomenon again in the Theseus myth in which he makes a relationship to Ariadne and uses her help, but then abandons her before he gets home. Although we have plenty of examples of how this breakdown can apply to the psychology of modern men, it also indicates the stage of development of the early Greek psyche. It is as though the feminine principle could not be assimilated in any complete way at that time because the society was still too close to the matriarchal phase and the masculine principle was not securely established. The masculine could not achieve a balance with the feminine, hence the most that could be done was to exploit the feminine principle and then drop it again. The result was that the anima turned into bitterness.

We may find in this an underlying explanation for the eventual fall of the ancient world: it could not assimilate the anima and the feminine principle. Certainly in Hellenistic times we note the development of a pervasive bitterness; a kind of rending sadness seems to run through most of Greek wisdom. Stoicism had an undercurrent of despair, and we see its ultimate expression in Sophocles, who gave vent to this prevalent feeling in these lines from *Oedipus at Colonus*: "Not to be born is, past all prizing, best; but when a man hath seen the light, this is next by far, that with all speed he should go thither, whence he hath come."[6] If that is the ultimate wisdom of life, it is a counsel of despair and reason enough for the decline of ancient civilization.

THESEUS AND ARIADNE   71

Theseus and Ariadne

The myths of Theseus and Perseus follow each other because the former concerns the encounter with the father monster and problems of the father complex, while the latter deals with the mother monster, the mother complex. It is helpful to compare the two myths.

Like other heroes, Theseus had a double parentage. He was fathered by King Aegeus, who was on a visit in Troezen, but according to some stories, his mother, Aethra, was visited by the god Poseidon. So his father on one hand was a god and on the other, a mortal. In either case, when Aegeus left for Athens he told Aethra he had deposited his sword and sandals under a great rock and that when his son was sixteen years old she was to take him to the rock. If he was able to lift it and retrieve the sword and sandals, he would prove that his parent was Aegeus, and he should then come and visit his father.

This echoes a characteristic theme in which the son, when he comes of age, is required to undergo some ordeal in order to receive his heritage from his father. Such a rite is involved in all of the basic choices of a young man, outstandingly in the determination of his vocation, the most crucial step he must take. He will be handicapped in deciding it unless he is in relation to his own inner masculine heritage. Does this mythological image apply to women and their choice of vocation? It is Erich Neumann's viewpoint,[7] as it is mine, that the hero myth also pertains to women, that these myths deal with the process of developing consciousness as such, and that process is symbolically masculine whether one is male or female.

After lifting the rock with ease, and recovering the sword and the sandals, Theseus set out on his journey to Athens to meet his father. Rather than taking the safe route directly by water, Theseus chose to go along the semicircular coast, which was known to be populated by criminals. He dreamed of performing heroic feats by engaging these public enemies.

On his way, Theseus had a series of ordeals in which he encountered various aspects of negative, unconscious masculinity. The first was a desperado named Periphetes, who waylaid travelers and clubbed them to death. Theseus grabbed his club and beat Periphetes to death. A feature of all his encounters was that the ruffians had done to them what they did to others, illustrating a basic psychological law: the way one behaves, so one is treated. That is true on the unconscious as well as on the conscious level. Periphetes was clubbed himself, and then Theseus made the club his own, so a bit of masculine power was won and was made available to the ego.

The next thug he met was a man named Sinis, the "pine bender." He would bend a pine tree to the ground, and then ask a passing traveler to hold it with him. As soon as the traveler would seize the tree, Sinis would release his grip and the traveler would be flung to his death. Theseus disposed of Sinis by that same method: he arranged it so that Sinis was thrown by his own tree. This is a strange image. Psychologically, it has something to do with distorting a natural growth tendency and then making use of the backlash of it. The bending of the natural tendency can only be held a short time and then it springs back to its original position. We might think of this as an image of excessive self-discipline that cannot last forever because it requires too much energy; sooner or later the natural forces exert their backlash and throw the ego off again. These images are the product of centuries of folk polishing, so to speak, and they have a lot to say about the human psyche.

Theseus then had to face Sciron, who was seated on a high rock where he forced passersby to wash his feet. While they complied he kicked them off the cliff into the sea where a great turtle devoured them. That would refer to the danger of succumbing to false humility, to a servile attitude, as the washing of the feet suggests. In other words, this chap took advantage of the individual's tendency to be obeisant or subservient, and then destroyed him for it. Theseus repaid him in kind.*

*At a superficial level, the image recalls Jesus' washing the disciples' feet. But the Biblical image belongs to a higher level of ego development and thus has a different meaning. The archaic Greek image applies to an earlier stage of ego development. The whole system of Christian virtues and the negation of the will is not really suitable for the young. One has to have something to sacrifice before giving up one's egocentricity means anything. It can often happen that the task of developing a sturdy, aggressive ego is bypassed by taking on those so-called self-sacrificial virtues prematurely, and then the life process is actually short-circuited rather than fulfilled.

Sciron was followed by Cercyon, a vicious fighter who would challenge each traveler and then crush him to death in his embrace. Theseus got the better of him by making use of the strategic principles of
wrestling, which he invented. He overcame Cercyon not by brute
force but by the application of conscious skill and inventiveness, suggesting that consciousness must use its own principles in dealing with
the unconscious forces and not try to meet the unconscious on its
own ground.

The final criminal the hero ran into is the best known: Procrustes.
This man captured travelers and laid them out on his bed. Those who
were too long for his bed he chopped off so they would fit, and those
who were too short he stretched out. This is such a striking image to
describe a well-known human tendency that it has become popular
in general usage. A procrustean bed is a rigid, preconceived attitude
that pays no attention to the living reality one is confronting, but
brutally forces it to conform to one's preconception. It describes the
danger of the ego's tendency to judge itself by alien standards, thus
suffering an amputation or distortion of its own natural reality, the
brutal effects of living by an unconscious "ought." Procrustes' bed is
an ought.

Finally arriving in Athens, Theseus was almost poisoned by
Medea, who was Aegeus' wife at that time. She told Aegeus that the
young man was a spy and Aegeus was about to become an accom-
plice to his murder when at the critical moment he caught sight of
the sword he had left for his son years before, and dashed the poison
cup from Theseus' hands. What does that mean? One interpretation
would be that just as the ego is completing one stage of relation to
the father principle, it almost succumbs to a poisonous regressive
maternal yearning within itself. In addition, we can say that there is
a reluctance on the part of the powers that be to let the new power
come into its own. The status quo wants to continue, and any newly
emerging force has to fight it out if it is not to be overcome.

Theseus, however, was recognized in time by his father and was
welcomed with open arms. So he reestablished his relation to the
father, the inner masculine principle to which he owed his being. But
no sooner had that happened than another trial presented itself to

him. In Crete, King Minos had once prayed for a demonstration of his special relation to the god Poseidon and he was given that recognition by the emergence of a beautiful white bull from the sea, with the understanding that the bull would immediately be sacrificed to Poseidon. But Minos thought the bull too beautiful to give back, so he sacrificed an inferior one. Poseidon, in retaliation, arranged that Minos' wife Pasiphaë should develop a passion for the white bull, and indeed she coupled with it and gave birth to the monster called the Minotaur, which had a bull's head and a human body, such a dreadful creature that it had to be hidden away in a labyrinth. The story tells us that when one takes for oneself what belongs to the divine powers, one breeds monsters. It does not go unnoticed when the ego, as Minos did, uses the transpersonal or instinctive energies for itself alone.

Then, because of offenses to the Cretan king (at this time, Athens was subject to Crete), it was decreed that every nine years Athens must supply seven youths and seven maidens to be fed to the Minotaur. Theseus arrived on the scene just when a new batch of youths and maidens was prepared to set sail to meet the monster, and he quickly offered himself as one of the tribute youths, with the intention of destroying the Minotaur.

Here is a picture of human contents being turned over to monster purposes, a state of affairs that had come about because the original bull from the sea was not voluntarily sacrificed to the god. The primitive instinctual energies that are signified by the bull were not sacrificed to a higher purpose, and the price of that failure was that human qualities represented by the tribute youths then had to be sacrificed to the bull. In place of a progressive developmental movement that would amount to an enlargement of consciousness, the more conscious humans were sacrificed to the less conscious Minotaur: a regressive movement.

This again brings up the symbolism of the bull. We know from archeological work in Crete that a remarkable sport existed there, a kind of bull dance in which acrobats would grab the horns of a bull and somersault onto and off its back, a prototype, clearly, of what has lasted into our own day as the bullfight. A human being's meeting and mastering the power of the bull seems to have a deep-seated psychological meaning. The bull stands for something that must be challenged and shown to be inferior to human power. Without this level of meaning, the elaborate rituals of confrontation with the bull cannot be understood psychologically.

Another important symbol system that made a great deal of the bull image was Mithraism, which became the major religion of the Roman legions in the first few centuries of this era, and according to some authorities, if Christianity had not supervened, would have become a worldwide religion. It had as its central image Mithras sacrificing the bull.

In psychological terms, the bull is the primordial unregenerate energy of the masculine archetype that is destructive to consciousness and to the ego when it identifies with it. Therefore, it must be sacrificed, and the sacrifice brings about a transformation, so that the energy symbolized by the bull serves another level of meaning. Seen this way it is not too much to say that the sacrifice or overcoming of the bull symbolizes the whole task of human civilization.

The Theseus myth is the story of encounters with both the good father and the father monster. Aegeus, the good father, helped his son to find him and then welcomed him. But when Theseus arrived in Crete he immediately encountered the negative father, King Minos. No sooner had the ship from Athens arrived than Minos espied one of the Greek maidens who appealed to him and was about to rape her on the spot. Theseus intervened, and in the altercation that followed Theseus proved his own relation to Poseidon by retrieving a ring that Minos threw into the sea. In this initial exhibition of his monstrous nature a certain correspondence between Minos and Minotaur is indicated and the very names suggest the similarity, making it clear that Theseus was confronting the masculine monster, the negative aspect of the father image, something that sons not uncommonly have to overcome in dealing with certain kinds of fathers.

It is interesting that although Aegeus was the good father, his consort, Medea, was destructive, a negative manifestation of the feminine associated with the positive father. In Crete there was just the opposite: Ariadne, the daughter of Minos, turned out to be helpful to Theseus—the bad father was accompanied by the good anima. This pattern has psychological implications. At a certain stage of development the positive relation that the son enjoys with the father hides a negative, dangerous aspect in the unconscious, signified by Medea. But as soon as it is realized that the relation to the father is not so purely positive as was thought, that actually the father can also be a negative and somewhat dubious figure, and as soon as that realization leads to appropriate behavior, then the positive anima (signified here by Ariadne) can emerge.

To meet the Minotaur, Theseus made his way into the labyrinth with the help of Ariadne, who was the Minotaur's half sister. It is as if she knew about him because she shared some of his qualities, and this reflects the characteristic theme of the anima linked with the monster in some way. Usually, the anima is held in bondage by a feminine monster, as in the myth of Perseus, but here we see a masculine monster that was not holding Ariadne in bondage but was associated with her; she was able to leave only upon his death. The Minotaur was successfully mastered with the help of the feminine, Ariadne providing a ball of thread, which was the essential guidance. We can consider Ariadne's thread as the thread of feeling; it is safe to confront one's unregenerate wrath and lust and instinctuality providing one can hold onto the thread of feeling relatedness that gives orientation and prevents one from getting lost in the labyrinth of the unconscious. We all have a minotaur in the labyrinth of the soul and until it is faced decisively it demands repeated sacrifices of human meanings and values. Thus, the principle of Eros or relatedness enabled Theseus to meet the Minotaur, and there is a parallel to this image in the medieval idea of the unicorn, that wild, irascible, and completely unmanageable creature that is tame only when in the lap of a virgin.

It is an evocative image, the labyrinth with the Minotaur prowling it. The implication of this particular myth is that at the stage in which Theseus negotiates the labyrinth there is a destructive aspect to the unconscious that requires a continuous tribute of human sacrifice—an intolerable state of affairs that cannot stop until the monster is overcome by a conscious encounter. Another way of looking at the myth is to see the Minotaur as a kind of guardian of the center. Surely the labyrinth is a representation of the unconscious, since it is that place where there is danger of getting lost. One of the aspects of the labyrinth, according to mythology, is the presence at the center of something very precious. That precious thing is not specified in the Theseus story, but it is implied in the person of Ariadne. Ariadne was the fruit that Theseus plucked from his experience with the labyrinth.

Theseus found the Minotaur by throwing down Ariadne's ball of thread, which rolled along unwinding itself, leading him to his destination—an image almost identical to one in an Irish fairy tale called "Conn-Eda," in which the hero cast an iron ball in front of him and followed it as it rolled on its way, leading him to a city where his various adventures took place. These are images of following the round object, the symbol of wholeness. The sphere is a prefiguration

FIG. 18. Theseus fights the Minotaur. (Detail of an Attic stamnos, c. 470 BC. Copyright British Museum, London.)

of the goal, the goal of totality. The ideas of wholeness and center are related to each other; they are part of the same symbolic nexus, so one might say that the round ball will automatically roll to the center. The fact that the sphere has an autonomous power to roll to the center suggests that it is also the path to individuation rolled up into a ball.

Theseus did as he was instructed by Ariadne and was able to overcome the Minotaur and find his way out of the labyrinth by means of the thread, the principle of relatedness. To understand what this motif could mean, one might imagine oneself in an agitated, enraged state, the Minotaur bellowing within. To confront one's fury will be safer, given the thread—a sense of human rapport and relatedness—so that one will not get lost in the rage and fall into identification with it.

Theseus left Crete with Ariadne, but he broke his promise to marry her. On the way back to Athens they stopped at the island of Naxos, and there are different versions of what happened there (indicating multiple symbolic meanings). One version is that Theseus tired of Ariadne; after all, she wasn't of any use to him anymore; he had achieved his purpose, and so he sailed off and left her. Another story is that the god Dionysus claimed her. The basic meaning, however, remains the same—the connection between the heroic aspect of the ego, Theseus, and the helpful anima could not be maintained. We witnessed a similar fate in the case of Jason and Medea, and we may assume that it signifies something of the same sort in the Greek psyche of that time: a stable, conscious assimilation of the anima could not be sustained. Although Ariadne was separated from the baleful shadow of her monstrous brother, she must remain related to the gods, so to speak—Dionysus, in her case—and was not yet ready for full participation in the human conscious realm. She had to remain largely an unconscious entity.

There is a further important episode of the story. When Theseus had departed from Athens, it was understood between him and his father that on his return, if he was successful, he would take down the black sails of his ship and hoist white ones. But he forgot about the agreement, and when his father spied the ship returning with its black sails, in his despair over what he took to be his son's failure, he threw himself off the cliff into the sea (which then took his name: the Aegean). We know that forgetting is meaningful, and it is part of the central significance of the myth that the father, Aegeus, should die. Theseus had now become the father, so to speak, overcoming his dependent relation to the father figure and the need for the father to mediate the masculine principle. With the death of the father the individual becomes directly related to the masculine principle himself.

Theseus appears again in a different role in the myth of Hippolytus, already touched on in the discussion of Aphrodite. There, Theseus played the bullish father in his relations with his son Hippolytus. As we saw, the young man had incurred the wrath and vengeance of Aphrodite by his devotion to Artemis and his rejection of love. She contrived that his stepmother, Phaedra, should fall in love with him, and when he rejected her advances, Phaedra told Theseus that he had molested her. That is an ancient theme, which arises when a younger man is living in the household of an older man but remains subordinate too long. His subordinate status is challenged symbolically when the man's wife takes him for a man, not a boy. The erotic complications initiate the necessary conflict between the younger and the older man.

Theseus was furious when he heard Phaedra's story. He believed her lie and prayed to Poseidon for revenge on his son. Poseidon sent a monster (some versions say a bull) which came out of the sea and frightened Hippolytus' horses when he was driving along the shore. He was tossed from his chariot and dragged to death. One way of seeing this is that Hippolytus had failed to meet the challenge of a new level of development, to realize himself as a mature erotic being. What he had consciously rejected came back in a negative form. Hippolytus' problem can be seen as the need to accept a fuller masculinity. At the immature level, the woman belongs to the father and Phaedra was the father's woman, hence Hippolytus dared not have a woman. The monster that came out of the sea and pursued Hippolytus can be seen as his own rejected masculine instincts that had not been faced, the very thing that Theseus faced in the Minotaur.

A patient once provided a vivid example of this theme. He had a bullish type of father who drove him to excel in various ways. This aggressiveness became interiorized and led to an inner pushing, a compulsive need to achieve, that went quite contrary to his own actual nature. His achievements were essentially hollow; he was living out the situation at the beginning of the Theseus story, submitting Athenian youths and maidens, internally, to the inner Minotaur. His real human meanings and human purposes were being fed to this brutal monster. On the night that he first decided to enter analysis he dreamed that he had to go through a maze, and at the end of the maze was the man who became his analyst. Exactly one year later to the day he had this dream:

> I was in a prison maze. Suddenly I saw an opening, the way through. I dashed down the long hall. I expected gunfire but I caught them by surprise. I crossed over the boundary. I knew I was free and now others would be also. It was as if I had performed a yearly ritual and now others would be free. I turned around and came back. As I walked back different people came toward me, as if they were coming out of their graves. They were old and young, men and women. I stopped each one and gave a deep, guttural sound. I was passing my freedom on to them.

Here the imagery is lifted wholesale out of the Theseus-Minotaur story, demonstrating that it is still operative symbolism—we are not just dealing with ancient history.

PERSEUS

According to one version of the Perseus myth, the father of Perseus' mother, Danaë, had been told by an oracle that a grandson would depose him. For that reason he had his daughter locked up in a brass-walled dungeon to keep her apart from men. But Zeus came to her in the chamber as a shower of golden rain by which she conceived Perseus. Another version had it that Danaë was seduced by her uncle, the hostile brother of her father, and because of this illegitimate conception, she was confined to the dungeon.

This is the ambiguity that appears repeatedly in the myths; like the double parentage theme, it poses a question about the origins of the hero, in this instance: is this a divine conception or is it an illegitimate one? Symbolically, the two are equivalent, because if the conception does not occur under human auspices, if it is not legitimized by human mores, then it is beyond the pale and takes on transpersonal meaning and the quality of divinity. We are on familiar ground if we think of the legends surrounding the birth of Christ. The canonical sources speak of the birth as a conception through the Holy Spirit, something like the shower of rain that came to Danaë. However, some legends current at the time had it that Mary became illegitimately pregnant by a Roman centurion.

The phenomenology of this image is important in dreams. Very often, early dreams dealing with the emergence of the Self depict the birth of an illegitimate child, or perhaps the birth of the child unites the races—maybe the child is half black and half white. Just those things that are beyond the pale and have been considered unacceptable by conscious standards accompany this birth, because the Self, by its very nature, transcends the rules of the ego.

It is worth noting how the ancient writers used the image of Danaë. Sophocles compared her to Antigone, who had dared to defy the tyrant Creon's decree that her dead brother, Creon's rebellious enemy, be left unburied. Burial was profoundly important to the ancient Greek mind, and Antigone proceeded to bury her brother despite the prohibition. In punishment she was walled up in a cave to perish. Sophocles then says this about her:

> Even thus endured Danaë in her beauty to change the light of day for brass-bound walls; and in that chamber, secret as the grave, she was held close prisoner; yet was she of a proud lineage, O my daughter, and charged with the keeping of the seed of Zeus that fell in the golden rain.[8]

Sophocles perceives that Antigone, in observing the divine law even when breaking man's law, was of the same nature as Danaë, who

kept the seed of Zeus to give birth to the hero Perseus. Psychologically, this image suggests that the birth of the individuation principle
is a dubious, ambiguous happening that entails being shut off from
the world at large. That was where Zeus encountered Danaë, shut
up in her brass-walled prison.

The birth of Perseus was characteristically followed by the hero's
rejection and abandonment. Perseus and his mother were cast into
the sea in a wooden chest, that is, were thrown into the unconscious,
with the assumption that they would perish and never be heard from
again. But in a miraculous way they landed on the island of King
Polydectes and there Perseus was brought up.

At a time when wedding gifts were being presented to the king, the
young Perseus, having nothing material to give, impetuously offered
the most extravagant service conceivable, namely to bring the king
the head of Medusa. The rashness and arrogance of the offer are
built into the myth so that we have to take them as expressing some
aspect of the individuation process: they apply to those stages where
a careful and deliberate weighing of the odds would never allow one
to get moving. If one had awareness in advance of what the prospects
were, psychological development would not get very far; it probably
would not get out of the womb. If Perseus was going to get somewhere, he had to make a daring leap. Then he was in for it; he had
to go through with it.

This brings us to the image of the Gorgon Medusa and how we
are to understand her. She is a common motif in Greek art. Greek
pottery and some of the older Greek sculpture and architectural
friezes show again and again the picture of the Gorgon, a ghastly
woman with teeth and tongue protruding and hair made up of writhing snakes. The prominence of this image of horror in early Greece
seems to portray what Nietzsche recognized so forcibly—the close-
ness of the Greek mind to the primordial depths out of which it had
recently emerged. Thus the Greek sensibility encompassed a keen
awareness of the horror of existence just below the surface, in a way
that we pampered, civilized people are usually spared, and it was
this that gave everything they did and everything they produced an
intensity that has never been equalled.

Medusa is an expression of that dreadful level of existence that, if one looks at it very long, has petrifying effects, and we are told that her image was so fearsome that to gaze upon it was to be turned into stone. She can, of course, also be seen as the negative mother archetype in its most terrifying aspect, able to immobilize the ego so that all that is moving and flowing and changing and spontaneous is utterly halted. This is the very image that the young person must encounter and deal with if he is going to make his way into life. He has to confront the horror of existence itself if his life is to proceed and develop. That is what Perseus did.

In this myth we find excellent examples of the helping deities of the Greek Pantheon. The two that came to Perseus' assistance were the typical helpers: by Hermes he was furnished with what is usually called a sickle, a blade with which to cut off Medusa's head, and from Athena he obtained a polished shield that was also a mirror, which enabled him to kill the Gorgon without having to look directly at her and become frozen in stone. There were some initial skirmishes with the female powers, since he had to seek out the Graiae in order to learn the way to Medusa. He stole the single eye and tooth they shared and so extracted from them directions to the three Gorgons. Finally, viewing Medusa by means of his mirror shield, he cut off her head. Instantly, out of the decapitated body sprang Chrysaor, a warrior who fathered future monsters, and more significantly, out of the severed head flew Pegasus, the winged horse. Here is a striking image of released libido. It is as if the decapitation of the Medusan horror had the effect of transforming the negative energy contained in her and releasing it into positive, creative power, signified by the horse, a symbol of physical energy that is at the same time winged. Pegasus later started the Peirene spring flowing, the spring of the Muses, with the powerful stamp of his moon-shaped hoof. So the arts derived from Pegasus' libido but their ultimate source was Medusa, since Medusa was the mother of Pegasus.

On his way back from his encounter with Medusa, Perseus came upon Andromeda, who was chained to a rock as a sacrifice for the crimes of her mother and was being threatened by a sea monster. Perseus destroyed the monster and released Andromeda—a typical

FIG. 19. Perseus attacks sleeping Medusa, looking away from her to Athena to avoid being turned
into stone. (Attic pelike, 5th century BC. Metropolitan
Museum of Art, Rogers Fund, 1945.)

image of the captive anima who must be freed. It is another version
of the freeing of Pegasus through the destruction of the Medusa monster, but on a more developed level, signifying the emergence of the
feminine relatedness function out of its instinctive, monstrous origins, here represented by the sea monster.

The reflecting shield of Athena is of particular importance, because
without that device Medusa could never have been faced and transformed. Given to the hero by the goddess, the embodiment of wisdom herself, Athena's mirror shield is an image of the civilizing
process, how it takes place, and how human consciousness is able to

overcome the primordial horror represented by the Medusa. The myth tells us that it takes a mirror to overcome or deal with the elemental terror of what exists in the unconscious. The primary feature of the mirror is its ability to produce images; it shows us what we otherwise cannot see for ourselves because we are too close to it. Without a mirror, for instance, we would never even know what our face looks like; since we are inside looking out, there can be no self-knowledge, even the elementary self-knowledge of what we look like, unless there is some device that can turn the light back on us, unless there can be a reflexive movement. The whole process of consciousness, in both the individual and collective sense, is served by an instrument that produces reflections, images giving us an objective sense of what we are. Athena's mirror, we should remember, is showing us an image of something we dare not look at directly; to grasp what we are dealing with, we need an image of it, we need to see it indirectly, which allows a more objective view. Surely it is not an accident that the term "reflection" refers to the specific capacity of human consciousness, the capacity to consider itself. That is the function of the mirror, and it is also the capacity of human consciousness to turn back on itself in self-critical, self-observing, self-scrutinizing reflection.

All art forms, literature, and drama are basically mirroring phenomena. Shakespeare tells us that in Hamlet's remark about the nature of the drama: "The purpose of playing . . . is to hold, as 'twere, the mirror up to nature; to show virtue her own feature, scorn her own image, and the very age and body of the time his form and pressure."[9] When we attend the theater we are, in effect, being mirrored. Jung called the theater the place where people work out their private complexes in public. We discover there what it is we react to, what it is that gets under our skin; we discover what is relevant to us. Those aspects of the theater and motion pictures that leave us cold will not serve the mirror function. The things we react to are mirroring some aspect of our inner nature and enable us to see it. The whole body of mythology serves that mirror function.

The mirror of Narcissus is an example of the risk lurking in the mirror. According to historians, Teiresias is supposed to have said,

"Narcissus will live a long life, providing he never knows himself"—
that is, providing he never looks into a mirror. But he did see his
reflection in a pool and his life was cut short. This speaks of the
danger that can come from seeing oneself prematurely, before one is
able to assimilate it.

It is instructive to consider the etymology of the word *mirror.* It
derives from the Latin *miror, mirare,* "to wonder at, to be aston-
ished," and therefore is cognate with such words as *miracle* and *ad-
mire.* The capacity to be amazed is connected to reflective
consciousness. The Latin word for mirror is *speculum,* from *specio,*
to look at or see. From that we have such words as *speculate* and
spectacles; various words associated with "scope," such as *telescope*
and *microscope,* also come from the same root.

The mirror is an interesting image in folklore. According to primitive thinking, the reflection in a mirror is actually one's soul. There
is thus something uncanny about mirrors that accounts for the super-
stition that breaking one brings bad luck. Gazing into the mirror was
not without risk, since one's soul might be snatched away while the
image was there. And covering mirrors after the death of a person
was often practiced to prevent the ghost of the departed one from
coming back through the glass or from dragging one into it. The
mirror, in other words, signified the threshold between this world
and the other world; Alice crossed this threshold in *Through the
Looking Glass* when she stepped into the mirror and passed over to
the other side, into the unconscious. Divination by mirrors was not
uncommon, giving rise to the original meaning of the term *speculate:*
to peer into a crystal ball or mirror in order to see into the future was
to speculate.

Mirror symbolism and imagery can be seen from two standpoints:
one is the collective function of the culture that we have just been
discussing, and the other is the individual process of psychological
development, and specifically the process of psychotherapy. A clear
parallel can be drawn between the process of development that takes
place in the personal analysis of the individual and the process of
cultural development that has occurred in the history of the race.
They are fundamentally of the same nature, one being the microcosm

of the other. Just as the cultural history of humankind requires that there be memory, a past and knowledge of that past, and a consequent sense of continuity, so in personal psychotherapy we start out with a history of the individual's past. One cannot exist as an aware, conscious being without remembering where one has come from, and what one has been. So a first procedure is to activate and stimulate the memory. As Santayana is supposed to have remarked about history in general, "He who does not remember the past is condemned to repeat it." That observation is certainly true of the individual: all those repressed experiences that have been blocked from one's individual memory, for whatever reason, will unfailingly be repeated again and again on an unconscious level until they are recollected and assimilated.

Then in psychotherapy we examine dreams. Dreams are the mirror that the unconscious throws up to us. The images we see in dreams are the reflections of our current state of being, and without those dreams we would have no way to perceive what we are. Dreams serve something of the same purpose for the individual that cultural forms, art, and literature serve for the collective. Individuals can also become their own artists and start painting their inner states or drawing them, or writing poems about them, thereby providing themselves with mirror images to enable themselves to see what they are. Active imagination serves the same mirror purpose.

The mirror function plays an important role in the therapist-patient relationship, which is one of the reasons that the relationship is so essential. Individuation does not proceed in a vacuum, because one needs not only an inner mirror but an outer one. We discover what we are to a significant extent by observing the effects we have on another; each of us serves a mirror purpose for the other, providing by our reactions, objective clues by which the other can increase his self-knowledge.

An impressive description of the significance of the mirror phenomenon is to be found in Schopenhauer, who in many respects can be regarded as the father of depth psychology. This passage is from *The World as Will and Representation:*

[It is] indeed wonderful to see how man, besides his life in the concrete, always lives a second life in the abstract. In the former he is abandoned to all the storms of reality and to the influence of the present; he must struggle, suffer and die like the animal. But his life in the abstract, as it stands before his rational consciousness, is the calm reflection of his life in the concrete, and of the world in which he lives. . . . Here, in the sphere of calm deliberation, what previously possessed him completely and moved him intensely appears to him cold, colorless and, for the moment, foreign and strange; he is a mere spectator [mirror-looker] and observer. In respect of this withdrawal into reflection, he is like an actor who has played his part in one scene, and takes his place in the audience until he must appear again. In the audience he quietly looks on at whatever may happen, even though it be the preparation of his own death (in the play); but then he again goes on stage and acts and suffers as he must.[10]

Psychologically speaking, what Schopenhauer is referring to is the ability to turn an unconscious complex, which possesses one, into an object of observation and knowledge. We could extend the analogy further and say that gaining such objectivity is really like struggling and suffering in the arena and then suddenly being transported from the arena to the spectator stand. That is what having a mirror is like. Being in the grip of the Medusan level of reality is transformed into the capacity to step aside and comprehend what one is dealing with from a distance. That is the basic requirement for developing consciousness.

6

The Trojan War

THE ILIAD, the epic of the Trojan war, appears to have been considerably more popular in antiquity than was *The Odyssey*. When Alexander the Great took a copy of Homer on his military campaigns, it was *The Iliad* that lay in his knapsack and at his bedside table, and this may stem from the fact that the Trojan War and *The Iliad* are primarily stories of the first half of life and its psychological issues.

The prologue to the war is evocative psychologically. The conflict grew out of what is known as the Judgment of Paris. Eris, the goddess of discord, threw a tantalizing golden apple into the assembly of the gods and goddesses and on it was written "for the fairest." Hera, Athena, and Aphrodite all claimed the designation, and it was decided that the cattleherd Paris, the young son of Priam, the Trojan king, would assume the task of deciding who was entitled to the apple—offering yet another example of the dictum attributed to the old philosopher from Ephesus, Heraclitus, who observed that "strife is the father of all things." Eris stirred up strife, and out of the strife emerged the Trojan War and all its consequences.

Paris was a young innocent. Though he was of noble birth, he had been sent to the countryside as a cattleherd. He signifies the ego to whom nothing has yet happened. Then out of the blue, Hermes, the messenger of the gods, presented him with an impossible task of judgment—to decide which of the three divinely beautiful goddesses was the fairest and should win the prize. Each sought to bribe him. Hera offered him the lordship of Asia and infinite riches; Athena promised him constant victory and wisdom; Aphrodite offered him the most beautiful woman of all to be his own; in short, Hera offered him power, Athena wisdom, and Aphrodite beauty. Paris tried to get out of it. He wanted to divide the apple into three pieces, but that was disallowed. He was forced to make a decision and he chose Aphrodite. The result was that Hera and Athena, in their rage at being rejected, initiated the Trojan War.

This story reflects a requirement of ego development. At a certain stage of psychological growth, a decision must be made as to what will be the highest value of the unfolding life. It is inevitable that if one is to develop a certain area of competence, one must make such a choice, and that means rejecting certain other possibilities. The myth tells us that having made such a choice, the rejected possibilities linger resentfully in the unconscious and eventually start trouble. It is really a tragic requirement that such a choice must be made if life is to unfold. Jung has reproduced an alchemical picture in *Psychology and Alchemy* with the title "The Awakening of the Sleeping King Depicted as a Judgment of Paris."[1] Paris, with the three naked goddesses in competition beside him, stands by a king sleeping on the ground. Paris is touching the sleeping king with his wand to wake him up. As he makes his judgment as to which feminine value will be most important, he is simultaneously awakening the sleeping king, the power of inner authority that had previously been unconscious. We can extrapolate to say that it does not matter which decision is made. Some people will give beauty the first value and reject the others, some may choose wisdom and still others power, but there will be a Trojan War no matter which is chosen because the neglected ones will react. In the myth, Aphrodite fulfilled her promise by giving Helen to Paris, who then abducted her from the palace of her husband, Menelaus, and took her to Troy where he lived. Hera and Athena then aroused the Greeks to fetch her back.

It is worthwhile to linger a little over the image of Helen. She is the classic anima figure of Western civilization. Gilbert Murray writes about her in his book *The Rise of the Greek Epic*:

> Think how the beauty of Helen has lived through the ages . . . it is now an immortal thing. And the main, though not of course the sole, source of the whole conception is certainly *The Iliad*. Yet in the whole *Iliad* there is practically not a word spoken in description of Helen . . . almost the whole of our knowledge of Helen's beauty comes from a few lines in the third book, where Helen goes up to the wall of Troy to see the battle between Menelaus and Paris. "So speaking, the goddess put into her heart a longing for her husband of yore and her city and her father and mother. And straightaway she veiled herself with white linen, and went forth from her chamber shedding a great tear. . . ." The elders of Troy were seated on the wall, and when they saw Helen coming, "softly they spake to one another winged words: 'Small wonder that the Trojans and the mailed Greeks should endure pain through many years for such a woman. Strangely like she is in face of some immortal spirit.' " That is all we know. Not one of the Homeric bards fell into the yawning trap of describing Helen, and making a catalogue of her features. She was veiled; she was weeping; and she was strangely like in face to some immortal spirit. And the old men, who strove for peace, could feel no anger at the war. . . . the weeping face of Helen [has behind it] not the imagination of one great poet, but the accumulated emotion, one may almost say, of the many successive generations who have heard and learned and themselves afresh recreated the old majesty and loveliness. They are like the watchwords of great causes for which men have fought and died; charged with power from the first to attract men's love, but now through the infinite shining back of that love, grown to yet greater power. There is in them, as it were, the spiritual life blood of a people.[2]

That is a description of an archetypal image written in 1907—before the theory of archetypes had been elaborated. The image of Helen runs through much of the literature and mythology of the Western world. She appears in the myth of Simon Magus, a Gnostic redeemer, who found Helen in a brothel in Tyre. She was, according to the myth, the incarnation of the fallen Sophia, the fallen wisdom of God. Simon Magus retrieved her from the brothel and took her on his travels. He was the prototype of the Faust legend, and Helen is present in all the versions of that story. In Christopher Marlowe's *The Tragedy of Doctor Faustus,* she enters after she has been summoned by Mephistopheles. Faustus exclaims:

> Was this the face that launched a thousand ships
> And burnt the topless towers of Ilium?
> Sweet Helen, make me immortal with a kiss.
> Her lips suck forth my soul, see where it flies!
> Come, Helen, come, give me my soul again.
> Here will I dwell for heaven is in these lips
> And all is dross that is not Helena.
> I will be Paris and for love of thee
> Instead of Troy shall Wittenberg be sacked.
> I will combat with weak Menelaus
> And wear thy colors on my plumed crest.
> Yea, I will wound Achilles in the heel
> And then return to Helen for a kiss.
> O thou art fairer than the evening air
> Clad in the beauty of a thousand stars!
> Brighter art thou than flaming Jupiter
> When he appeared to hapless Semele.
> More lovely than the monarch of the sky
> In wanton Arethusa's azured arms
> And none but thou shall be my paramour![3]

Shortly, he had to pay the price and be consigned to hell. An ominous implication is already in the lines "brighter art thou than flaming Jupiter when he appeared to hapless Semele." Semele was the mother of Dionysus, who insisted on seeing Zeus, or Jupiter, in his true form and was blasted to death by the sight. And that in effect is what happened to Faust. He took Helen for his own pleasure, and when an archetype is approached with such an attitude, it destroys.

The image of Helen runs throughout Goethe's *Faust* as the basic motivation of the whole story. In part one Gretchen is a personal representation of Helen, and in part two Helen herself appears and at the very end takes on the final glorification of the eternal feminine. One can say that Goethe's *Faust* completes *The Iliad* so far as the image of Helen is concerned because the anima is there redeemed and recognized as divine, which becomes evident in the final lines of part two. After Faust has arrived in heaven, these are the lines, as Louis MacNeice translates them:

> All you tender penitents,
> Gaze on her who saves you—
> Thus you change your lineaments
> And salvation laves you.
> To her feet, each virtue crawl,
> Let her will transcend us;
> Virgin, Mother, Queen of all,
> Goddess still befriend us!
>
> All that is past of us
> Was but reflected;
> All that was lost in us
> Here is corrected;
> All indescribables
> Here we descry;
> Eternal womanhood
> Leads us on high.[4]

This is the ultimate apotheosis of Helen through Western literature.

In *The Iliad,* eternal womanhood, at a more primitive level, leads men into a bloody battle. Jung has spoken of the anima image as the archetype of life, and its dynamism is to lead one into life, and often, as well, into painful, complicated, ambiguous situations.

Helen had a sister. According to the story, Helen was fathered by Zeus in the form of a swan, and her sister Clytemnestra came from a human father, Tyndareus. These sisters were married to brothers,

Helen to Menelaus and Clytemnestra to Agamemnon. The bulk of the retribution for Helen's abduction and all its consequences fell upon Agamemnon and Clytemnestra rather than upon Helen and Menelaus. Agamemnon and Clytemnestra represent the human level of the unfolding sequence, and Helen—and by contiguity with her, Menelaus—represent the archetypal or divine component, who are not touched. Menelaus and Helen returned home and lived on uneventfully. Agamemnon and Clytemnestra lived out the tragic dimension.

Helen was plucked out of her Mycenean palace and abruptly everything changed. Suddenly the anima was no longer safely ensconced in the familiar surroundings. Suddenly she disappeared, spirited away to Troy; hence, all Greece must be mobilized to bring her back. This situation could well be seen psychologically as an anima projection, in which the anima instead of being experienced internally is discovered elsewhere. The effect is to activate the ego to repossess her, Agamemnon as the leader of the Greek forces here signifying the ego. As this mobilization proceeded, even the heroes attempted to evade the draft. Odysseus for instance had been told by an oracle that if he went to Troy he would not get back for twenty years. When he heard that the recruiters were coming, he feigned madness. He was found plowing a field with an ass and an ox yoked together. The ruse was detected when his son was put in front of the plow and Odysseus veered away to prevent killing him, proving he was not mad. Psychologically, we might say that the difficult call to individuation cannot be avoided by such wiles because denial of it involves killing the child, the child symbolizing the future potentiality that will be destroyed if the task is not accepted.

The expedition assembled under the leadership of Agamemnon was preparing to set sail at Aulis when the wind suddenly began blowing in the wrong direction, as if the spirit was against them—the objective transpersonal spirit. A soothsayer informed them that Artemis had been offended and demanded the sacrifice of Agamemnon's daughter Iphigeneia, and after strenuous attempts to evade such a crime, she was given over for sacrifice.

Here we are told that for a masculine enterprise of the magnitude of the campaign against Troy, a young feminine element of the psyche must be sacrificed. This corresponds to a certain stage of psychological development in young men in which the feminine component, and feminine values, must be depreciated if the masculine principle is to find the energy to function. At this stage, to be buffeted by two contrary values operating simultaneously is immobilizing, like contrary winds; one can't get out of the original harbor that way. It generally happens on a purely automatic, instinctive basis that the young man at a certain level belittles womanhood and femininity. As the myth tells us, doing so is a crime, a grave crime that brings grave consequences, which the myth reveals as the story later unfolds. It works in the short run, the first half of life, but not later on when the man has to meet the consequences of his earlier decisions.

The image of Iphigeneia can also operate in the psyche of the woman, but it is damaging. An example of this was a woman who in childhood had been the butt of jokes and mistreatment from the men in her environment, a kind of scapegoat of the masculine ego to maintain its own illusory sense of importance. The result was that, in a certain sense, she became identified with Iphigeneia and her image. She once dreamed that her portrait was being painted. Intended to express her inner soul, it bore the title "Iphigeneia Looking Out to Sea."

When Agamemnon arrived home ten years later, he was forced to meet the consequences of the sacrifice that had enabled him to go to Troy. Clytemnestra was waiting to take revenge on him for it, and in Aeschylus' *Agamemnon* it is made quite clear that the basic sin for which he must die is what the Greeks called *hybris*. Upon his arrival his wife sought to have him walk on a lavish purple cloth that had been spread out from his chariot to the palace. Agamemnon protested in these words:

Know, that the praise which honor bids us crave,
Must come from others' lips, not from our own:
See too that not in fashion feminine
Thou make a warrior's pathway delicate;
Not unto me, as to some Eastern lord,

Bowing thyself to earth, make homage loud.
Strew not this purple that shall make each step
An arrogance; such pomp beseems the gods,
Not me. A mortal man to set his foot
On these rich dyes? I hold such pride in fear,
And bid thee honor me as man, not god.[5]

But despite those protests he succumbed and trod the purple into the palace and to his death.

The Greeks had great fear of *hybris*. In its original usage the term meant a kind of wanton violence or passion arising from pride—in psychological terms, inflation. It is the human arrogance that appropriates to man what belongs to the gods, or in psychological terms appropriates to the ego what belongs to the transpersonal level of the psyche. *Hybris* is the transcending of proper human limits, and Gilbert Murray has this to say about it:

> There are unseen barriers which a man who has reverence [the Greek word is *aidos*] in him does not wish to pass. *Hybris* passes them all. *Hybris* does not see that the poor man or the exile has come from Zeus [as Philemon and Baucis could see]: *Hybris* is the insolence of irreverence: the brutality of strength. . . . It is a sin of the strong and proud. It is born of . . . satiety—of "being too well off;" it spurns the weak and helpless out of its path. . . . [It is] the typical sin condemned by early Greece.[6]

If we read the Agamemnon story as a typical and more or less inevitable process in psychological development, it means that the experience of *hybris* is more or less unavoidable. As other material indicates, just the presumption for an ego to come into existence at all and to claim itself as a separate center of conscious being is replete with *hybris,* and this psychological fact then links with the imagery of original sin, which is a symbolic example of *hybris*.

It appears that the forerunner of *The Iliad* as we know it was originally a poem called "The Wrath of Achilles," and the opening of *The Iliad* indicates that Achilles is really the central figure. It begins this way:

The wrath of Peleus' son [Achilles], the direful spring
Of all the Grecian woes, O Goddess, sing!
That wrath which hurled to Pluto's gloomy reign
The souls of mighty chiefs untimely slain;
Whose limbs unburied on the naked shore
Devouring dogs and hungry vultures tore.
Since great Achilles and Atrides strove,
Such was the sovereign doom and such the will of Jove.[7]

In these opening lines it almost sounds as though Achilles' wrath caused the war in the first place, but what it did cause was a prolongation of that war, resulting in far more casualties than would otherwise have been the case. Achilles was an invulnerable hero, or almost so, a gift of his mother Thetis, who following his birth dipped him in the River Styx, a process that protected him except for the place on his heel where she held on to him.

How do we interpret that psychologically? It can be said that Achilles represents the life and fate of the psychic factor that is invulnerable by virtue of having experienced total maternal love and acceptance in childhood. Achilles is a mother's boy in the best sense of that term and there is a lot of psychological evidence to indicate that total loving acceptance on the part of the mother does indeed convey a kind of psychological invulnerability, generating self-assurance and confidence in one's own worth that is built in; one is dipped in invulnerability. Freud was an example of the Achilles experience: he was the firstborn and favorite son of his adoring mother, who repeatedly told him about predictions of his greatness. In later life Freud wrote, "A man who has been the indisputable favorite of his mother keeps for life the feeling of a conqueror, that confidence of success that often induces real success."[8] That sounds all very enviable, of course, but there is still the heel, because whatever is conveyed by a process other than one's own must have some defect. To become whole, one cannot have anything given entirely from the outside; indeed, only a monster would be totally invulnerable. Rather it is Achilles' vulnerability that saves his humanity, so to speak. As *The Iliad* proceeds, it becomes clear that Achilles' vulnerability, psychologically speaking, lay in his sulky resentments. At the outset of the war, Agamemnon was obliged to give up a prize of battle, his favorite concubine, whom he was required by the gods to return to her father, leaving him in the intolerable position of being womanless when all his men enjoyed such company. He solved the problem by appropriating Achilles' concubine, stirring Achilles to such resentment that he refused to participate any further in the war and retreated to sulk in his tent.

Here we have a second case, on another level, of the loss of a woman influencing the war, which had been set off by the loss of Helen. Achilles' vulnerability came from his inability to accept the objective authority of others. Agamemnon makes that point when he says, speaking of Achilles:

> . . . that imperious, that unconquered soul,
> No laws can limit, no respect control.
> Before his pride must his superiors fall,
> His word the law, and he the lord of all?
> Him must our hosts, our chiefs, our self obey?
> What king can bear a rival in his sway?[9]

In his refusal to recognize the authority of Agamemnon, Achilles came to grief on the power problem. Since he could not oppose Agamemnon on realistic grounds, he opposed him by what we would call an anima mood, a sulky, resentful withdrawal. And this indeed fits the psychology of a mother's favorite, inasmuch as he becomes accustomed to having everything he wants, making it difficult, if not impossible, for him to subordinate his world to the objective authority of others. Achilles' response, in effect, was to subvert the whole Greek enterprise by personalizing its purposes.

Achilles eventually lost his life by being pierced in his one weak spot, but *The Iliad* does not go into that. *The Iliad* as a work of art has its own beginning and end, and it ends differently; it ends in a resolution. Although it is a frightfully brutal work, what starts out as the wrath of Achilles is resolved in a reconciliation between Achilles and Priam. Achilles finally returned to the fighting through another personal motivation: his closest friend, Patroclus, was killed.

So his wrath against Agamemnon was redirected to Hector, who had killed Patroclus. Hector, the foremost champion of the Trojans and son of Priam, the king, was slaughtered and his body was ignominiously dealt with by the vengeful Achilles. But aged Priam picked his way through the enemy lines, with the help of Hermes, and arrived as a suppliant at Achilles' tent.

Priam begged Achilles to be allowed to ransom back the body of his son, something that meant a great deal in those times. These are the concluding lines, in effect the end of *The Iliad* and the reconciliation. Old Priam is talking to Achilles and telling him why he has come:

"For him [Hector], through hostile camps I bent my way,
For him thus prostrate at thy feet I lay;
Large gifts, proportioned to thy wrath, I bear;
Oh hear the wretched and the gods revere!

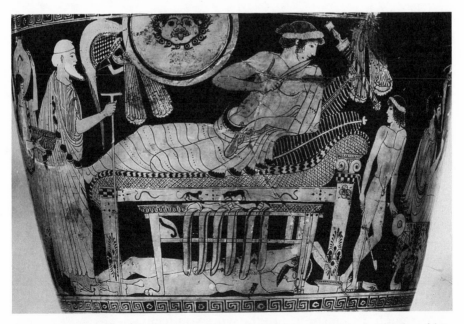

FIG. 20. Old King Priam approaches Achilles to ransom the body of his son, Hector, that lies beneath Achilles' couch. (Detail of an Attic skyphos, c. 480 BC. Kunsthistorisches Museum, Vienna.)

Think of thy father and this face behold!
See him in me, as helpless and as old,
Though not so wretched: there he yields to me,
The first of men in sovereign misery.
Thus forced to kneel, thus groveling to embrace,
The scourge and ruin of my realm and race;
Suppliant my children's murderer to implore,
And kiss those hands yet reeking with their gore!"
These words soft pity in the chief inspire,
Touched with the dear remembrance of his sire.
Then with his hand (as prostrate still he lay),
The old man's cheek he gently turned away.
Now each by turns indulged the gush of woe
And now the mingled tides together flow:
This low on earth, that, gently bending over;
A father one, and one a son, deplore:
But great Achilles different passions rend,
And now his sire he mourns, and now his friend.
The infectious softness through the heroes ran;
One universal, solemn shower began;
They bore as heroes, but they felt as man.
Satiate at length with unavailing woes,
From the high throne divine Achilles rose;
The reverend monarch by the hand he raised;
On his white beard and form majestic gazed,
Not unrelenting; then serene began
With words to soothe the miserable man.
"Alas! what weight of anguish hast thou known?
Unhappy prince! Thus guardless and alone
To pass through foes and thus undaunted face
The man whose fury has destroyed thy race?
Heaven sure has armed thee with a heart of steel,
A strength proportioned to the woes you feel.
Rise then: let reason mitigate our care:
To mourn avails not: man is born to bear.

Such is, alas! the gods' severe decree:
They only are blessed and only free."[10]

This is the resolution, in which their mutual humanity was experienced in their mutual flow of tears and their realization that they were in the same relation to the gods. It was a *coniunctio,* a coming together of opposites. Starting out with a war between opposites, the sad reconciliation was the conclusion.

7

Odysseus

WHILE THE Trojan war can be seen as an outgoing, a leaving of one's house in the morning and going out into the arena and tumult of life, the journey narrated in *The Odyssey* represents a return, a coming back to where one started. The two can be seen as analogous to the two halves of life: the first half, in which the ego progressively realizes its power and expands its functions and capacities, and the second half, in which the ego turns more and more inward to realize the source from which it comes.

Many of the heroes of the Trojan War met adventure on the way home, but the legendary voyage of Odysseus became the central one. Psychologically, his series of experiences represents confrontations with the unconscious in one form or another that he had to meet and deal with effectively if he was to reach his home in Ithaca. The encounters express the nature of the unconscious as the ego experiences it in the search for the realization of the Self, and they constitute the classic metaphor for the process of discovering the inner source; hence the word *odyssey* comes to mind when one is contemplating a quest for an ultimate value, which is what the word has come to signify.

We learn the attitude Odysseus started out with at the city of the Cicones, his first stop after leaving Troy:

From Ilios the wind bore me and brought me to the Cicones, to Is-marus. There I sacked the city and slew the men; and from the city we took their wives and great store of treasure, and divided them among us, that so far as lay in me no man might go defrauded of an equal share. Then verily I gave command that we should flee with swift foot, but the others in their great folly did not hearken. But there much wine was drunk, and many sheep they slew by the shore, and sleek kine of shambling gait. Meanwhile the Cicones went and called to other Ci-cones who were their neighbors, at once more numerous and braver than they—men that dwelt inland and were skilled at fighting with their foes from chariots, and, if need were, on foot. So they came in the morning, as thick as leaves or flowers spring up in their season; and then it was that an evil fate from Zeus beset us luckless men, that we might suffer woes full many. They set their battle in array and fought by the swift ships, and each side hurled at the other with bronze-tipped spears. Now as long as it was morn and the sacred day was waxing, so long we held our ground and beat them off, though they were more than we. But when the sun turned to the time for the unyoking of oxen, then the Cicones prevailed and routed the Achaeans, and six of my well-greaved comrades perished from each ship; but the rest of us escaped death and fate.[1]

Here the course of the battle is described as fluctuating with the course of the sun, and as an introductory image for *The Odyssey,* it can refer to what the work symbolizes as a whole. This was really Odysseus' first discovery that the warrior's reliance on ego power would not solve the problems of the return journey, a lesson he was to be given many times.

The incident displays the ruthless frame of mind that Odysseus set out with. He and his men were warriors inflated by their victory at Troy, but that attitude now proved to be inappropriate. The change is indicated by the fact that until midday they prevailed over the enemy, but after midday the enemy prevailed, and the incident clearly indicates that we are now dealing with the second half of life. We can compare this image in *The Odyssey* and this way of understanding it with what Jung has to say about the transition between the first and the second half of life. He writes:

Experience shows us that the basic cause of all the difficulties of this transition is to be found in a deep-seated and peculiar change within the psyche. In order to characterize it I must take for comparison the daily course of the sun—but a sun that is endowed with human feeling and man's limited consciousness. In the morning it rises from the nocturnal sea of unconsciousness and looks upon the wide, bright world which lies before it in an expanse that steadily widens the higher it climbs in the firmament. In this extension of its field of action caused by its own rising, the sun will discover its significance; it will see the attainment of the greatest possible height, and the widest possible dissemination of its blessings, as its goal. In this conviction the sun pursues its course to the unforeseen zenith—unforeseen, because its career is unique and individual, and the culminating point could not be calculated in advance. At the stroke of noon the descent begins. And the descent means the reversal of all the ideals and values that were cherished in the morning. The sun falls into contradiction with itself. It is as though it should draw in its rays instead of emitting them. Light and warmth decline, and are at last extinguished.[2]

As the second half of life proceeds, the ego must accept its own diminishment and its relative unimportance in relation to the Self. We can take this to be the message Odysseus received from his initial exploit as he started on his way home—on his path downward from the zenith.

After weathering a storm, Odysseus and his men landed on the island of the Lotus-eaters. Lotus-eating has peculiar effects, as Homer describes:

> Whosoever of them ate of the honey-sweet fruit of the lotus, had no longer any wish to bring back word or to return, but there they were fain to abide among the Lotus-eaters, feeding on the lotus, and forgetful of their homeward way.[3]

When his sailors took up lotus-eating, they refused to continue their journey and had to be forcibly returned to the ship with great weeping and protesting, a picture of falling under the enchantment, ease, and sweet voluptuous idleness of the unconscious in its slothful aspect, something of which Tennyson evokes in his poem "The Lotos-Eaters":

> They sat them down upon the yellow sand,
> Between the sun and the moon upon the shore;
> And sweet it was to dream of Fatherland,
> Of child, and wife, and slave; but evermore
> Most weary seemed the sea, weary the oar,
> Weary the wandering fields of barren foam.
> Then someone said, "We will return no more"
> And all at once they sang, "Our island home
> Is far beyond the wave; we will no longer roam."[4]

Once the individual has relinquished established ego standards, which one must do on one's homeward journey—and which Odysseus was obliged to do after the defeat by the Cicones—this regressive danger enters the picture.

The lotus-eating attitude might also correspond to what Jung has called the aesthetic attitude toward the unconscious, a state of mind that enjoys the imagery of the unconscious passively as one might watch a motion picture. Concerning this problem Jung says:

> It often happens that the patient is quite satisfied with merely register-ing a dream or fantasy, especially if he has pretensions to aestheticism. He will then fight against even intellectual understanding because it seems an affront to the reality of his psychic life. [A little like the lotus-eating sailors, who fought to avoid being returned to the ships.] Others try to understand with their brains only, and want to skip the purely practical stage. And when they have understood, they think they have done their full share of realization. That they should also have a *feeling relationship* to the contents of the unconscious seems strange to them or even ridiculous. Intellectual understanding and aestheticism both produce the deceptive, treacherous sense of liberation and superiority which is liable to collapse if feeling intervenes. Feeling always binds one to the reality and the meaning of symbolic contents, and these in turn impose binding standards of ethical behavior from which aestheti-cism and intellectualism are only too ready to emancipate themselves.[5]

In effect, lotus-eating is a metaphor for the aesthetic or intellectual approach to the unconscious that Jung describes.

On the island of the Cyclopes Odysseus and his men met Polyphemus, a primitive giant with a single wheel-like eye in the center of his forehead. Having discovered a large, commodious cave, which they entered, they found themselves to be prisoners of Polyphemus when the giant came home and threw a great stone across the entrance of the cave. He was a man-eater and proceeded to eat two of Odysseus' men for supper and another two for breakfast. They eventually escaped by getting Polyphemus drunk and blinding him by jamming a pointed stake into his eye, and then tying themselves under the bellies of his sheep, slipping out of the cave, in effect, disguised as sheep.

What does all this mean? In describing the land of the Cyclopes, Homer says:

> [The Cyclopes are] an overweening and lawless folk, who, trusting in the immortal gods, plant nothing with their hands nor plough; but all these things spring up for them without sowing or ploughing, wheat, and barley, and vines, which bear the rich clusters of wine, and the rain of Zeus gives them increase. Neither assemblies for council have they, nor appointed laws, but they dwell on the peaks of lofty mountains in hollow caves, and each one is lawgiver to his children and his wives, and they reck nothing one of another.[6]

What is described amounts to a state of paradise, and it parallels quite closely Hesiod's description of the Golden Age, which he characterized this way:

> [The golden race of men] lived like gods without sorrow of heart, remote and free from toil and grief. . . . They had all good things; for the fruitful earth unforced bare them fruit abundantly and without stint. They dwelt in ease and peace upon their lands, with many good things, rich in flocks, and loved by the blessed gods.[7]

The original paradise state corresponds to the meaning of the single, round, wheel-like eye. These giants are identified with the circular mandala image. They are an expression of the original unconscious wholeness before the birth of the opposites. It is the state into which we are born, what Neumann calls the uroboros,[8] the condition in which the newborn ego experiences itself as the center and totality of things; it is the source of feelings of infantile omnipotence. To fall victim to that original unconscious, God-identified wholeness is analogous to being devoured by or succumbing to a kind of monster. The crew escaped this peril by destroying that original single eye, that original wholeness. Beyond that, in order to flee they had to identify with utter innocence and harmlessness. All willfulness had to be disposed of, at least temporarily, if they were to escape under the bellies of the sheep.

When Odysseus was in Polyphemus' cave, he had given his name as "no man," as if he could not assert his identity there. When back at sea, distanced from the isle on which Polyphemus was raging, he could not resist the insolence of shouting, "In case anybody asks you who put your eye out, tell them it was Odysseus from Ithaca!" From presumed safety he declared his own identity and that cost him a heavy price; not only was he almost struck by a huge stone that Polyphemus hurled out blindly in the direction of the sound, but also knowing Odysseus' name enabled Polyphemus to pray to his father Poseidon to avenge his blinding. Odysseus was thus plagued by Poseidon all the way home with recurrent storms and troubles. Odysseus' taunt reestablishing who he was could simply be called a bad mistake. However, it is part of the myth, and that suggests that although temporary anonymity may be necessary, unless one's unique individuality is reasserted, no matter what the cost, the Self will never be realized. Hence it was essential that Odysseus declare his identity and then take the consequences.

Nonetheless, he acted in an inflated way, by taunting Polyphemus, and the indication that he got caught in inflation lies in the following episode. At the island of Aeolus the god of winds presented him with a bag containing the four winds, which were to be released only one by one, and gradually, so that he would have each wind he needed to get him home safely. The sailors, however, thinking the bag contained gold, freed all the winds at once, whereupon a violent storm erupted, blowing them back to where they started. The whole inflated pretension collapsed because the dark side, represented by the sailors' greed, took over. Later in the land of the Laestrygonians, who were cannibal giants, the men on eleven of the twelve ships were eaten. The devouring aspect of the unconscious took a heavy toll.

Following this, Odysseus underwent a formidable experience on the island of Circe, an enchantress, who by drugs and magic turned men into animals, in particular into pigs. When a party of Odysseus' men exploring the island accepted Circe's hospitality and were turned into pigs and placed in her pigpens, Odysseus set out to rescue them. On his way he met Hermes, the guide and bringer of wisdom in time of trouble. Hermes gave him an antidote to Circe's drug, a plant called moly, and this advice:

> [Circe] will mix thee a potion, and cast drugs into the food; but even so she shall not be able to bewitch thee, for the potent herb that I shall give thee will not suffer it. And I will tell thee all. When Circe shall smite thee with her long wand, then do thou draw thy sharp sword from beside thy thigh, and rush upon Circe, as though thou wouldst slay her. And she will be seized with fear, and will bid thee lie with her. Then do not thou thereafter refuse the couch of the goddess, that she may set free thy comrades, and give entertainment to thee.[9]

And so it happened. Odysseus followed the instructions and Circe immediately changed, turning friendly and helpful and, indeed, becoming Odysseus' lover. About the herb called moly, Odysseus said:

> [Hermes] gave me the herb, drawing it from the ground, and showed me its nature. At the root it was black, but its flower was like milk. Moly the gods call it, and it is hard for mortal men to dig, but with the gods all things are possible.[10]

This image of the moly herb, which has a black root and a white flower, which cannot be dug up by mortal men but only by gods, is an image in *The Odyssey* that precedes very widespread allegorical use in later antiquity. It was employed by the Stoics, the Neoplatonists, and the early Christian fathers, each in the context of their own ideas. The image seems to have attracted projections from the unconscious; it was used as an image of salvation, even from very different standpoints and in different contexts. It was thought of as whiteness that grows out of the dark roots of existence. Cleanthes, the Stoic philosopher, said: "Moly is an allegorical representation of the logos, by whose power the lower instincts and passions are made weaker."[11] The Gnostics used the image. Clement of Alexandria identified Christ with Hermes and the Gospel with the moly that Hermes provided. Heraclitus, a scholar of the Augustan period, had this to say about moly:

> [Insight or consciousness] is most appropriately represented by moly. This is a gift which can only be given to human beings, and to very few human beings at that. The most essential thing about moly is that its root is black and its flower milk-white. Now the first steps toward insight, which is a kind of simultaneous comprehension of all that is good, are rough, unpleasant and difficult, but when a man has bravely and patiently surmounted the trials of these beginnings, then, as he progresses, the flower opens to him, as in a gentle light.[12]

The plant appears again in alchemy, where it is associated with the philosophers' stone. In some texts it is made synonymous with the golden flower of alchemy.

Moly can best be understood as a symbol of the Self, which is indicated chiefly by the fact that it is a union of opposites, the black root and the white flower. It carries with it the idea that contact with wholeness is a saving factor. Circe, as a personification of the unconscious, would have a destructive and regressive effect if one encountered her without moly in one's possession. Related to one's own wholeness, one would not fall victim to her machinations. Further, not only did Odysseus manage to neutralize Circe, he caused her to become helpful rather than hindering. This, too, we see in regard to the psychology of the unconscious. If the ego is able to face up to what seems threatening and destructive in the unconscious, the very process of the encounter can make that unconscious energy available in a way helpful to the ego. At the same time, the myth reminds us that mortal men cannot pluck the moly plant out of the ground; the gods have to do it. So its help comes by grace and not by the will of the ego.

The most crucial episode of *The Odyssey* follows in Book Eleven and is entitled "The *Nekyia*," a term that refers to the Underworld, the land of the dead. After Odysseus had spent some time with the transformed, helpful Circe, he was told that before he could proceed he must make a trip to the Underworld, where he was to consult the spirit of the dead sage Teiresias as to how to make his way safely home. On first hearing this, Odysseus sank into despair: ". . . my spirit was broken within me, and I wept as I sat on the bed, nor had my heart any longer desire to live and behold the light of the sun. [Finally] . . . I had had my fill of weeping and writhing. . . ."[13]

A repetition of this grief and despair can be found at the start of three other great stories of the soul's journey into the Underworld. In *The Divine Comedy* Dante describes the beginning of his *nekyia*:

> Midway upon the journey of our life
> I found that I was in a dusky wood;
> For the right path, whence I had strayed, was lost,
> Ah me! How hard a thing it is to tell
> The wildness of that rough and savage place,
> The very thought of which brings back my fear!
> So bitter was it, death is little more so.[14]

Faust, too, opens on this note. We find Faust lamenting his fate and even contemplating suicide:

> Oh couldst thou, light of the full moon,
> Look now thy last upon my pain,
> Thou for whom I have sat belated
> So many midnights here, and waited.
> Oh! Am I still stuck in this jail?
> This God-damned dreary hole in the wall,
> Cooped up among these heaps of books,
> Gnawed by worms, coated with dust . . .

Infinite nature, where can I tap thy veins?
Where are thy breasts, those well-springs of all life
On which hang heaven and earth,
Towards which my dry breast strains?
They well up; they give drink,
But I feel drought and dearth.[15]

This is followed shortly afterward by Faust's pact with Mephistopheles, which is another image to express the descent into the unconscious.

And in yet another expression of the *nekyia*, this one four hundred years later, the opening lines of *Moby-Dick* sound the note of despair and emptiness and hopelessness:

Call me Ishmael. Some years ago—never mind how long precisely—having little or no money in my purse, and nothing in particular to interest me on shore, I thought I would sail about a little and see the watery part of the world. It is a way I have of driving off the spleen and regulating the circulation. Whenever I find myself growing grim about the mouth; whenever it is a damp, drizzly November in my soul; whenever I find myself involuntarily pausing before coffin warehouses, and bringing up the rear of every funeral I meet; and especially whenever my hypos get such an upper hand of me, that it requires a strong moral principle to prevent me from deliberately stepping into the street, and methodically knocking people's hats off—then, I account it high time to get to sea as soon as I can. This is my substitute for pistol and ball. With a philosophical flourish Cato throws himself upon his sword; I quietly take to the ship. There is nothing surprising in this. If they but knew it, almost all men in their degree, some time or other, cherish very nearly the same feelings towards the ocean with me.[16]

It is clear that the experience is a fundamental one, but Book Eleven of *The Odyssey* marked the first clear expression of the image that finds perhaps its fullest conscious realization in depth psychology.

Circe gave Odysseus precise directions to the Underworld: he was to sail to the edge of the world, to Oceanus, and when he came to the right place he was to dig a pit, sacrifice rams, and allow the blood of the sacrifices to flow into the pit, thus attracting the spirits from Hades, who could not speak until they had first drunk blood. Here is an apt image to describe how the unconscious is activated. If we understand the dead spirits as contents of the unconscious that are apparently dead and inactive, only their empty forms present, then to vitalize them so the ego can hear what they have to say, energy must be poured into them. This energy can only come from what is available to consciousness; if a certain kind of attention has to be applied to the images of the imagination, it has to be taken from somewhere else. It is obtained by a sacrifice; one may have to sacrifice interest in certain external things, for example, to muster the libido to pour into the unconscious and activate it.

Odysseus was directed to stand guard over the blood and allow only those spirits that he wanted to make contact with to drink of it. (The psychological process does not enjoy such control over what content is activated.) The first spirit to arise was a recently dead comrade; Odysseus' latest experience of death was the one that was most readily available. Next to appear was his dead mother, and then came Teiresias, who gave him detailed advice on how to get back to Ithaca. A parade of other figures followed. We can recognize this symbolic scene as an original representation of what Jung called active imagination, a method that uses fantasy to explore the contents of the unconscious.

So pregnant is the image of the *nekyia* that Jung has suggested that the word be used as a technical term for the descent into the unconscious. Nietzsche used the image in describing certain experiences of his own:

I, too, have been in the underworld, like Odysseus, and shall be there often yet; and not only rams have I sacrificed to be able to speak with a few of the dead, but I have not spared my own blood. Four pairs it was that did not deny themselves to my sacrifice: Epicurus and Montaigne, Goethe and Spinoza, Plato and Rousseau, Pascal and Schopenhauer. With these I must come to terms when I have long wandered alone; they may call me right and wrong; to them will I listen when in the process they call each other right and wrong. Whatsoever I say, resolve, or think of for myself and others—on these eight I fix my eyes and see their eyes fixed on me.

May the living forgive me that occasionally *they* appear to me as shades, so pale and somber, so restless and, alas, so lusting for life— while those men then seem so alive to me, as if now *after* death, they could never again grow weary of life. But *eternal aliveness* is what counts.[17]

Nietzsche is telling us that he relates more to the spirits of these dead philosophers than to his contemporaries, and certain sacrifices of external adaptation had to be made to produce the blood that called them into reality. He is directly identifying with Odysseus during his *nekyia.*

Rome produced its own version of the *nekyia,* one that seems so close a parallel to the Greek that some scholars have insisted that in *The Aeneid* Virgil copied Homer—that is, since Odysseus had to undergo such an experience, Aeneas had to have one, too. But it might be more accurate to assume that both epics were written out of the depths and touched the same archetypal patterns. Aeneas was obliged to make a journey to the Underworld to consult his dead father, just as Odysseus was directed to meet Teiresias. First, Aeneas had to find a golden bough in the sacred grove, which would serve as a kind of passport, and as in *The Odyssey,* a sacrifice had to be made. Virgil says,

> And here the priestess for the slaughter set
> Four bullocks, black ones, poured the holy wine
> Between the horns, and plucked the topmost bristles
> For the first offering to the sacred fire,
> Calling on Hecate, a power in heaven. . . .
> The warm blood caught in bowls. . . .[18]

After that sacrifice, the entry into the Underworld began, led by a sibyl, a priestess-anima who served the function of psychopomp. A section of the text will give the flavor of Aeneas' descent. The sibyl exhorts him:

"Courage Aeneas; enter
The path, unsheath the sword. The time is ready
For the brave heart." She strode off boldly, leading
To the open cavern and he followed.
Gods of the world of spirit, silent shadows,
Chaos and Phlegethon, areas of silence,
Wide realms of dark, may it be right and proper
To tell what I have heard, this revelation
Of matters buried deep in earth and darkness!
Vague forms in lonely darkness, they were going
Through void and shadow, through the empty realm,
Like people in a forest when the moonlight
Shifts with a baleful glimmer and shadow covers
The sky, and all the colors turn to blackness.
At the first threshold, on the jaws of Orcus,
Grief and avenging cares have set their couches,
And pale diseases dwell, and sad old age,
Fear, evil-counselling hunger, wretched need,
Forms terrible to see, and death, and toil,
And death's own brother sleep, and evil joys,
Fantasies of the mind, and deadly war,
The Furies' iron chambers; Discord, raving,
Her snaky hair entwined in bloody bands.
An elm tree loomed there, shadowy and huge,
The aged boughs outspread, beneath whose leaves
Men say the false dreams cling, thousands on thousands.
And there are monsters in the dooryard: centaurs,
Scyllas of double shape, the beast of Lerna
Hissing most horribly. Briareus, the hundred-handed giant,
A chimera, whose armament is fire, harpies and gorgons,
A triple-bodied giant. In sudden panic
Aeneas drew his sword, the edge held forward,
Ready to rush and flail however blindly,
Save that his wise companion warned him, saying
They had no substance, they were only phantoms
Flitting about, illusions without body.[19]

This is the same counsel given in *The Tibetan Book of the Dead,* where the dead soul is constantly reminded, "Do not succumb to panic, these are only phantoms of your own mind." Aeneas made the mistake of concretizing the forms he encountered, as if they were entities that could be dealt with in realistic form, and of course his sword was useless with them. He had mistaken psychic for physical reality, which corresponds to what happens in the case of projection, where one thinks of an unconscious image as an external fact rather than as an internal one.

The grand vision that Aeneas eventually came to is relevant psychologically. When he met his father, Anchises, Aeneas wanted to know what the transcendent world was like, and Anchises gave him a lesson in the ultimate nature of things:

First, my son, a spirit
Sustains all matter; heaven and earth and ocean,
The moon, the stars; mind quickens mass, and moves it.
Hence comes the race of man, of beast, of wingèd
Creatures of air, of the strange shapes which ocean
Bears down below his mottled marble surface.
All these are blessed with energy from heaven;
The seed of life is a spark of fire, but the body
A clod of earth, a clog, a mortal burden.
Hence humans fear, desire, grieve and are joyful,
And even when life is over, all the evil
Ingrained so long, the adulterated mixture,
The plagues and pestilences of the body
Remain, persist. So there must be a cleansing,
By penalty, by punishment, by fire,
By sweep of wind, by water's absolution,
Before the guilt is gone. Each of us suffers
His own peculiar ghost. But the day comes
When we are sent through wide Elysium,
The Fields of the Blessed, a few of us, to linger
Until the turn of time, the wheel of ages,
Wears off the taint and leaves the core of spirit

Pure sense, pure flame. A thousand years pass over
And the god calls the countless host to Lethe
Where memory is annulled and souls are willing
Once more to enter into mortal bodies.[20]

The point here, which has great relevance to what is encountered in modern psychological experience, is that the purpose of the descent into the Underworld is to gain something that is missing in the upper world, some piece of information, some wisdom. This is symbolized at times by a jewel or other object of value, but what generally is come upon is a transpersonal principle, such as Aeneas found when his father unfolded the nature of things. Once the ego has had an encounter with the transpersonal standpoint, it is transformed. Now related to meaning, life is no longer empty or absurd, but is perceived as part of a larger and meaningful pattern. The basic message in Anchises' revelation to Aeneas is that a spirit sustains all matter and meaning lies embedded in all experience. The passage owes much to the "Vision of Er" in Plato's *Republic,* to be taken up later.

Odysseus had been warned by Teiresias to be wary of the Island of the Sirens. The Sirens sang so sweetly and seductively that any sailor who heard them was irresistibly lured to their island only to be destroyed on the rocky shore. Teiresias cautioned Odysseus that if he wanted to listen to the Sirens' song he must have his men bind him to the mast and plug their ears with wax. What Odysseus heard the Sirens sing, according to Homer, was this:

"Come hither, as thou farest, renowned Odysseus, great glory of the Achaeans; stay thy ship that thou mayest listen to the voice of us two. For never yet has any man rowed past this isle in his black ship until he has heard the sweet voice from our lips. Nay, he has joy of it, and goes his way a wiser man. For we know all the toils that in wide Troy the Argives and Trojans endured through the will of the gods, and we know all things that come to pass upon the fruitful earth."[21]

It was not a sexual but a spiritual and intellectual seduction, appealing to the desire for omnipotent knowledge. The Sirens were thought

FIG. 21. Odysseus hears the sirens' song while safely bound to the mast of his ship. A siren, failing to lure him to his destruction, plunges into the sea in despair. (From an Attic stamnos, c. 475 BC. Copyright British Museum, London.)

to have total foreknowledge, and following that sweet song, one would be made omniscient. In Plato the Sirens were the ones said to create the music of the spheres, the celestial harmony generated by the revolutions of the planets.[22] They offered transcendent knowledge, knowledge of the archetypal world, and the hazardousness of listening to them corresponds psychologically to the danger in being lured into the unconscious out of desire to know about the mysteries. For an undeveloped ego to succumb to that lure exposes it to dissolution in the archetypal. As the myth warns, it is safe to listen to the sources of divine knowledge only when one is solidly lashed to the mast of reality. Peril lies in the exploration of the unconscious, for the archetypal symbolism and images can be exciting and provocative, opening up vistas that seem enlarging and valuable; yet they can overwhelm any ego that is not grounded in reality. One sees that risk in the tendency to seek the transcendent experience in drugs, out of curiosity and the desire to know more, without the body of sufficient reality commitment. Jung provides testimony on this point in what he says about his own encounter with the unconscious in *Memories, Dreams, Reflections:*

> Particularly at this time, when I was working on the fantasies, I needed a point of support in "this world," and I may say that my family and my professional work were that to me. It was most essential for me to have a normal life in the real world as a counterpoise to that strange inner world. My family and my profession remained the base to which I could always return, assuring me that I was an actually existing, ordinary person. The unconscious contents could have driven me out of my wits. But my family, and the knowledge: I have a medical diploma from a Swiss university, I must help my patients, I have a wife and five children, I live at 228 Seestrasse in Küsnacht—these were actualities which made demands upon me and proved to me again and again that I really existed, that I was not a blank page whirling about in the winds of the spirit, like Nietzsche. Nietzsche had lost the ground under his feet because he possessed nothing more than the inner world of his thoughts—which incidentally possessed him more than he it. He was uprooted and hovered above the earth, and therefore he succumbed to exaggeration and irreality. For me, such irreality was the quintessence of horror, for I aimed, after all, at *this* world and *this* life. No matter how deeply absorbed or how blown about I was, I always knew that everything I was experiencing was ultimately directed at this real life of mine. I meant to meet its obligations and fulfill its meanings.[23]

This was the mast to which Jung was bound, which enabled him to make his own *nekyia* and listen to those siren songs without being destroyed by them.

The image has many echoes. Even in medieval times Odysseus lashed to the mast was compared to Christ on the cross. The alchemical image of the mercurial serpent nailed or transfixed to a tree relates to the operation of *coagulatio* in alchemy, which has to do with being bound to the manifestation of a concrete reality and hence fully embodied in a particular and concrete form; only in such a situation is it safe to listen to the music of the spheres. Any seeking after religious

experience that does not take these facts into account can be a perilous seduction, which is also the message of the encounter with the
Sirens.

Odysseus and the crew next had to pass between Scylla and Charybdis, that famous image of the opposites. Charybdis, a female
monster, manifested itself as a sucking whirlpool, while Scylla was a
doglike creature that dwelled in a cave on a high cliff and would seize
sailors off the decks of ships and devour them. There was no way
through but down the middle, avoiding the whirlpool on one side
and the man-eater on the other, indicating explicitly that an identification with either of a pair of opposites or a one-sided imbalance is
fatal to the journey. This concept of pursuing the middle way, the
mean, expressed in the early myths was picked up by the philosophers and writers and became a central dictum in the wisdom of the
ancient Greeks—in Plato, for instance: "[Let man know] how always
to choose . . . the life that is seated in the mean and shun the excess
in either direction, both in this world so far as may be and in all the
life to come, for this is the greatest happiness for man."[24] And again:
"The right road in life is neither pursuit of pleasure nor yet unquali-
fied avoidance of pain, but that contentment with the intermediate
condition to which I have given the name of *graciousness*. . . ."[25] The
middle way, the way between the opposites, is the way of development. To identify with either side of a pair of opposites can be para-
lyzing. Caught in such a conflict, one's development cannot proceed,
for one is living out an archetypal role instead and one's own unity,
which lies between and beyond the opposites, cannot be realized.
This wisdom derives from the built-in compensatory function of the
psyche and is manifested repeatedly in dreams; whenever the conscious personality tends to get one-sided or imbalanced, the unconscious tends to right the balance. There is always the striving for the
middle way, the way between Scylla and Charybdis.

An episode follows on the island of Helios where the cattle of the
sun were stolen by Odysseus' men. Teiresias had warned against this
too, and Odysseus had so instructed his men, but they grew hungry
and killed a few of the cattle. Their punishment was a furious storm
in which all were destroyed but Odysseus, who at this point was

finally stripped down to nothing. He had lost his last ship, he had lost all of his men, and he was almost sucked back into Charybdis. Grabbing a fig tree, he barely managed to escape that fate and was left alone, drifting on the water, finally to be cast up on Calypso's isle. Such was the result of this final act of *hybris,* of appropriating the god's property.

Calypso proved to be a positive figure. She gave him food and drink and love; he even had children by her and was happy for a while. He had escaped with his life, and Calypso promised him immortality and eternal youth, which aroused in him a profound temptation to abandon his journey home. Eventually, however, his life on Calypso's isle began to feel like imprisonment and Calypso would not let him go. Rescue came again in the form of Hermes who brought an order from Zeus releasing him. He built a raft, made provision, and was sent on his way—to be greeted by a final terrifying storm. His raft was destroyed and death seemed certain, but in the midst of that utter peril, the sea goddess Ino gave him her veil to help him survive the raging sea. It is an image of the situation Hölderlin speaks of: "Where danger is/There also grows the rescuing power."[26] At the very moment of greatest unconscious turmoil, when the sea was ready to swallow up Odysseus and his whole enterprise, from the sea itself came Ino, who took pity on him, a rescue from the unconscious by itself, so to speak.

Odysseus finally landed on the island of the Phaeacians, received their hospitality, and told them his whole story. After they had heard it all they agreed to help him home by providing one of their miracle ships that guided themselves. The Phaeacians said to him:

> Tell me the name by which they were wont to call thee in thy home, even thy mother and thy father and other folk besides, thy townsmen and the dwellers round about. For there is no one of all mankind who is nameless, be he base man or noble, when once he has been born, but parents bestow names on all when they give them birth. And tell me thy country, thy people and thy city, that our ships may convey thee thither, discerning the course by their wits. For the Phaeacians have no pilots, nor steering-oars such as other ships have, but their ships of

themselves understand the thoughts and minds of men, and they know the cities and rich fields of all peoples, and most swiftly do they cross over the gulf of the sea, hidden in mist and cloud, nor ever have they fear of harm or ruin.[27]

The image implies that Odysseus had reached a point similar to that of coming within the field of a powerful magnet: once one gets within a certain range the rest happens automatically. It suggests psychologically that Odysseus had made contact with an autonomous process of development, which took over. The offer of the ship was prefaced by the demand to tell his name, as if the establishment of one's identity was a crucial element, and this is another familiar dream motif. When a certain point has been reached, some special demonstration of identity is required, whether it be a passport or a signature or a fingerprint, and that, of course, is what the individuation process is about—a full realization of one's identity.

The final aspect of the saga to be noted concerns the location of his landing at Ithaca: a cove at a place that was called the Cave of the Nymphs. Homer describes it as follows:

There is in the land of Ithaca a certain harbour of Phorcys, the old man of the sea, and at its mouth two projecting headlands sheer to seaward, but sloping down on the side toward the harbour. These keep back the great waves raised by heavy winds without, but within the benched ships lie unmoored when they have reached the point of anchorage. At the head of the harbour is a long-leafed olive tree, and near it a pleasant, shadowy cave sacred to the nymphs that are called Naiads. Therein are mixing bowls and jars of stone, and there too the bees store honey. And in the cave are long looms of stone, at which the nymphs weave webs of purple dye, a wonder to behold; and therein are also ever-flowing springs. Two doors there are to the cave, one toward the North Wind, by which men go down, but that toward the South Wind is sacred, nor do men enter thereby; it is the way of the immortals.[28]

Though the image of this cave is not elaborated especially in Homer, the ancient imagination projected great importance onto the

Cave of the Nymphs. In an essay on the symbolic meaning of Homer's cave, Porphyry[29] perceives it as the place where heaven and earth meet, where souls descend from heaven by the northern door and have bodies woven around them, so to speak, and depart by the southern door when they shed their bodies to return to their celestial home. This cave, that is to say, is the navel of the world, where spirit and matter interpenetrate, and all these images are part of the phenomenology of the Self. Hence, Odysseus had finally arrived at the transition place between heaven and earth. When we consider that this is an ancient projection of the image, we cannot but find significance in the fact that Odysseus should be landed on his home island at the place that was thought to be the boundary line between the transpersonal realm and the personal realm—psychologically, the border between the objective psyche and the personal psyche. The return leads to the reunion with Penelope, and the final image is that of the *coniunctio,* the union of Odysseus and his long-lost wife.

8

The Tragic Drama

OEDIPUS

CERTAIN OF the myths that were crucial to the Greek psyche came to be acted out in religious ritual and later in the drama. The tragic drama seems to have emerged out of a ritual in the worship of Dionysus—the acting out, in some simple way, of his myth. While watching the drama, the spectators became identified with the mythical happening being portrayed, which allowed them to participate briefly in the archetypal level of reality. We know from psychotherapeutic experience that an encounter with the archetypal dimension can have healing and transformative effects, and in this respect drama has many parallels to dreams, serving something of the same purpose for the collective psyche that dreams do for the individual. Aristotle described the effect of watching tragedy as a catharsis in which one has the opportunity to release the emotions of pity and fear.[1] Just as a possessed person is calmed by the playing of frenzied music, so sad and anxious people are relieved by seeing the emotions that grip them acted out. Thus, the play functions as a mirror that provides an image to objectify the inner affect.

Modern psychology can add another aspect to our understanding of the significance of tragic drama. The tragic hero depicts the ego undergoing individuation, which in part is a tragic process. We can define individuation as the ego's progressive awareness of and relation to the Self, but, as Jung has pointed out, "the experience of the self is always a defeat for the ego,"[2] and a defeat for the ego is experienced as tragedy.

Gilbert Murray has given us a valuable description of the origin and basic features of classical tragedy.[3] It is his view that Greek tragedy originated as the ritual reenactment of the death and rebirth of the year-spirit (equated with Dionysus) and that this reenactment had four chief features. First came an *agon,* or contest, in which the protagonist, the representative of the year-spirit, finds himself in conflict with darkness or evil. There followed a *pathos,* or passion, in which the hero undergoes suffering and defeat, after which a *threnos,* or lamentation, for the defeated hero was enacted. And finally a *theophany* pictured a rebirth of life on another level with a reversal of emotion from sorrow to joy. This sequence compares closely with the ritual drama of Osiris and of Christ, each of which possesses the characteristic features of the death and rebirth of the year-spirit. In later Greek tragedy the theophany all but disappears, remaining only as a hint. In psychological terms we can say that the tragic process involves the overcoming of the ego, or the defeat of the conscious will, as preparation for the final epiphany, the appearance of the Self.

The Shakespearean scholar A. C. Bradley speaks of the tragic hero in terms of a fatal flaw. This corresponds to what Jungian psychology knows as the problem of the inferior function, a recognition of the fact that one side of the circle of the personality always remains undeveloped and open to the depths. The so-called "fatal flaw" is thus a typical feature of the individual psyche. Bradley also speaks of Shakespeare's tragic heroes as having "a fatal tendency to identify the whole being with one interest, object, passion, or habit of mind."[4] This, likewise, is a well-known psychological phenomenon in which the ego identifies with the superior function; but that identification with its greatest strength is ultimately followed by a descent into its greatest weakness.

Bradley has a description of tragedy that is relevant here. He writes:

> [In Shakespearean tragedy, man] may be wretched and he may be awful, but he is not small. His lot may be heart-rending and mysterious, but it is not contemptible. The most confirmed of cynics ceases to be a cynic while he reads these plays. And with this greatness of the tragic hero (which is not always confined to him) is connected, secondly, what I venture to describe as the center of the tragic impression. This central feeling is the impression of waste. With Shakespeare, at any rate, the pity and fear which are stirred by the tragic story seem to unite with, and even to merge in, a profound sense of sadness and mystery, which is due to this impression of waste. "What a piece of work is man," we cry, "so much more beautiful and so much more terrible than we knew! Why should he be so if this beauty and greatness only tortures itself and throws itself away?" We seem to have before us a type of the mystery of the whole world, the tragic fact which extends far beyond the limits of tragedy. Everywhere, from the crushed rocks beneath our feet to the soul of man, we see power, intelligence, life and glory, which astound us and seem to call for our worship. And everywhere we see them perishing, devouring one another and destroying themselves, often with dreadful pain, as though they came into being for no other end. Tragedy is the typical form of this mystery, because the greatness of soul which it exhibits, oppressed, conflicting and destroyed, is the highest existence in our view. It forces the mystery upon us, and it makes us realize so vividly the worth of that which is wasted. . . .[5]

Bradley expresses vividly how the fourth phase of the ritual drama of the year-spirit, the theophany, while no longer in the drama itself, is transferred to the experience of the spectators. In viewing the tragedy, the spectators become aware of the transpersonal worth of man; they become the ground, so to speak, on which the theophany is experienced.

This ancient sequence of four stages—the contest, the defeat, the lamentation, and the theophany—is found in all important processes of psychological development and certainly in every psychotherapeutic process that delves at all deeply. At times a given phase may repeat itself; as long as the *agon* ends in success, for example, the process will not go any further, having been short-circuited, so to speak; the happy victor leaves the scene little knowing he has missed the main experience. But no one has perpetual success; sooner or later defeat does come, and that then leads to further development and to the possibility of completion of the sequence.

Let us examine the two Oedipus plays of Sophocles, *Oedipus the King* and *Oedipus at Colonus,* as examples of the tragic process. These plays hold particular significance to depth psychology because Oedipus became the first archetype to be discovered when Freud made the important observation that this archetype can give rise to a complex, the Oedipus complex. Since then we have learned that any archetypal image can manifest itself as a personal complex in the individual psyche, showing that other tragic figures besides Oedipus can be at the root of psychic complexes.

Oedipus the King begins in the middle of the story and requires an introduction to bring the reader up to that moment. Because of an oracle's prophecy that he was destined to kill his father and marry his mother, Oedipus was abandoned at birth and left for dead, but unbeknownst to his parents, a shepherd rescued him and took him to the king of Corinth, who adopted him and reared him in his own house. Some fifteen years before the opening of the play, Oedipus learned from the oracle at Delphi that he was destined to murder his father and marry his mother. He determined never to return to Corinth, whose king and queen he believed to be his parents. His wanderings eventually brought him by chance to the city of Thebes, where his true father and mother reigned. On the way there, he had brawled over the right of way with an old man in a carriage and in a fit of temper killed him, and arriving at Thebes, he found the city in an uproar because the king, Laius, had gone on a journey and never returned. Meanwhile, a female monster, the Sphinx, had taken up a position on a rock outside Thebes and was strangling the inhabitants one by one when they were unable to answer her riddle. Oedipus answered it, and the Sphinx threw herself from the rock. The citizens

FIG. 22. Young Oedipus ponders the sphinx's riddle.
(Detail of an Attic cup, c. 470 BC. Vatican Museum, Rome.
Photo: Alinari/Art Resource, New York.)

in gratitude made Oedipus their king and he married Jocasta, their widowed queen. No one, least of all Oedipus, suspected that Jocasta was his real mother and that the old man he had killed on the road was Laius, his father, thus fulfilling the prophecy. There followed fifteen years of apparent prosperity, but then, because the gods were disgusted by the corrupt situation, Thebes was struck by a plague. The people, led by their priests and elders, flocked around the great Oedipus imploring him to save them. This is where the play begins.

As the drama opens Oedipus is in his prime. He signifies the successful, confident ego that thinks it has met life well, overcome its problems (represented by the Sphinx), and has nothing more to fear. Concerning this overconfidence, Jung writes,

[The] tragic consequences . . . could easily have been avoided if only Oedipus had been sufficiently intimidated by the frightening appearance of the "terrible" or "devouring" Mother whom the Sphinx personified. . . . Little did he know that the riddle of the Sphinx can never be solved merely by the wit of man. . . . A factor of such magnitude cannot be disposed of by solving a childish riddle. The riddle was, in fact, a trap which the Sphinx laid for the unwary wanderer. Overestimating his intellect in a typically masculine way, Oedipus walked right into it . . .[6]

Oedipus' illusory state of well-being is interrupted by an outbreak of the plague. He is told:

> . . . look upon the city, see the storm
>   that batters down this city's prow in waves of blood:
> The crops diseased, disease among the herds.
> The ineffectual womb rotting with its fruit.
> A fever-demon wastes the town
>   and decimates with fire, stalking hated
>   through the emptied house where Cadmus dwelled:
> While poverty-stricken night grows fat on groans and elegies in
>   Hades' Halls.[7]

The theme of the diseased or barren land, which also appears in the beginning of the Grail legend, has its psychological counterpart in a state of depression, a loss of energy, interest, and life-meaning, a neurotic condition requiring action, and Oedipus, the ego, is called upon to do something about it.

> So, Oedipus, you most respected king,
> we plead with you to find for us a cure:
> Some answer breathed from heaven, perhaps,
>   or even enlightenment from man . . .
>
> Mend the city, make her safe. . . .
> Be equal to your stature now.
> If king of men (as king you are),
>   then be it of a kingdom manned and not a desert.[8]

Oedipus resolutely sets out to discover what is wrong. In psychological terms, a distressing problem that needs attention has arisen, the first appearance of a symptom. Realizing he must act, the individual may enter psychotherapy. In the play Oedipus sends Creon to consult the oracle at Delphi. The message that comes back is, "Banish the murderer of Laius." In psychotherapy, the unconscious is consulted, perhaps by examining dreams, and the answer that comes may be to bring the guilty one to justice, which is to say in other words, the shadow, the unknown dark side of the personality, must be made conscious. Oedipus readily agrees to this procedure; the evil is his own, but he still naively imagines himself innocent.

Teiresias the seer is called; that is, the unconscious is consulted again on another level. Replies to his questions are gradually forced out of Teiresias by Oedipus, but when the incriminating evidence first appears Oedipus accuses Teiresias and Creon of the crime—the first emerging awareness of the shadow leads to its projection. But that cannot be sustained, and Oedipus' origin gradually unfolds as he seeks it out. The shepherd who rescued him as an infant is found and questioned and Oedipus learns that he is, in fact, Jocasta's child. Hearing the dreadful truth, Jocasta disappears into the palace. Finally and cataclysmically insight bursts upon Oedipus. Awareness of his identity and his guilt conjoined rushes in on him and he cries:

Lost! Ah lost! At last it's blazing clear.
Light of my days, go dark. I want to gaze no more.
My birth all sprung revealed from those it never should;
Myself entwined with those I never could;
And I the killer of those I never would.[9]

He rushes into the palace, sees Jocasta, who has hanged herself, and blinds himself with the pins of Jocasta's brooches. The symbol of blindness plays an important role in the Oedipus dramas. It is paradoxical. At the moment that Oedipus sees himself as he really is, he blinds himself. Earlier Teiresias had said to him,

I'm blind, you say; you mock at that!
I say you see and still are blind—appallingly:

Blind to your origins and to a union in your house.
Yes, ask yourself where you are from?
You'd never guess what hate is dormant in your home
  or buried with your dear ones dead,
    or how a mother's and a father's curse
Will one day scourge you with its double thongs
  and whip you staggering from the land.
It shall be night where now you boast the day.[10]

When Oedipus can see physically, he is blind psychologically; and as he comes to see psychologically, he becomes blind physically. Echoing this paradoxical symbolism is the fact that Teiresias the seer is blind, indicating that sight of one kind is deleterious to sight of another kind—as though inner and outer sight work reciprocally.

Let us consider the nature of Oedipus' insight. He discovered literally that he had murdered his father and married his mother, probably the worst crimes of which ancient man could conceive. Psychologically, the precise content of the sinfulness is not essential; the content can vary in different circumstances and still the basic Oedipus experience is the same. In a single moment, Oedipus discovered both his identity and his guilt, thus experiencing for himself the teaching of traditional Christianity, that man is a miserable sinner. In psychological terms, Oedipus was overwhelmed by a sudden realization of the shadow, and the intensity of his reaction indicates that he had encountered not the personal shadow but the archetypal shadow. There is an echo of Oedipus' self-horror in John Bunyan's description of his own self-loathing:

But my original and inward pollution, that was my plague and my affliction. . . . By reason of that, I was more loathsome in my own eyes than was a toad; and I thought I was in God's eyes too. Sin and corruption, I said, would as naturally bubble out of my heart as water would bubble out of a fountain. . . . I could have changed heart with anybody. I thought none but the Devil himself could equal me for inward wickedness and pollution of mind. . . . I was both a burden and a terror to myself; nor did I ever so know, as now, what it was to be weary of my life, and yet afraid to die. How gladly would I have been anything but myself! Anything but a man! And in any condition but my own.[11]

This must reflect quite closely what Oedipus felt when the shattering truth dawned on him. It is the experience of extreme shadow awareness that potentially can lead into its opposite, as Meister Eckhart insisted, saying that if I find myself completely empty, totally devoid of worth, God has to flow in and fill me up; He doesn't have any choice. Martin Luther expresses a similar idea when he says:

> God works by contraries. So that a man feels himself to be lost in the very moment when he is on the point of being saved. When God is about to justify a man, he damns him. Whom he would make alive he must first kill. God's favor is so communicated in the form of wrath that it seems furthest when it is at hand. Man must first cry out that there is no health in him. He must be consumed with horror. This is the pain of purgatory. . . . In this disturbance salvation begins. When a man believes himself to be utterly lost, light breaks.[12]

Oedipus the King ends with the total defeat of Oedipus. There is no theophany, which is reserved for *Oedipus at Colonus,* the second part of the drama and remarkably similar to part two of *Faust.* As the second play opens, Oedipus has long been banished from Thebes and is wandering from place to place, guided by his daughter. Characteristic of one stage of individuation, the theme of the wanderer is widely found. Cain was condemned to wander. According to legend, Elijah and the Wandering Jew were both required to wander homelessly until the Messiah appeared, and in Gnostic thought the whole earthly life of man is considered to be a banishment from his heavenly home. Psychologically, the state of banishment and wandering is a necessary intermediate condition in the process of individuation: one cannot find a durable relation to the inner center, the Self, until one has been deprived of comfortable outer containments and identifications.

After his own long wanderings, Oedipus came at last to a sacred spot close to Athens. He was now a sage and holy man, a precious sacred entity. His two sons, battling one another for Thebes, both sought his approval because an oracle had pronounced that whoever gained it would prevail. The oracle had also declared that the tomb of Oedipus would bless the land it was on. He had become a sacred object, a living theophany. In this passage blind Oedipus describes the holy power of his tomb:

> Come, listen, son of Aegeus,
> I lay before you now a city's lasting treasure.
> There is a place where I must die,
> And I myself unhelped shall walk before you there.
> That place you must not tell to any living being:
>   not where it lurks, nor where the region lies,
>   if you would have a shield like a thousand shields
>   and a more perpetual pact than the spears of allies.
>
> No chart of words shall mark that mystery.
> Alone you'll go, alone your memory
>   shall frame the spot.
> For not to any person here,
>   not even to my daughters so beloved,
>   am I allowed to utter it.
> You yourself must guard it always.
> And when your life is drawing to its close,
>   divulge it to your heir alone
>   and he in turn to his, and so forever.
>
> This way you will keep your city safe
>   against the Dragon's seed, the men of Thebes,
>   though many a state attack a peaceful home,
>   though sure be the help from heaven (but exceeding slow)
>   against earth's godless men and men gone mad.
> Be far from you such fate, good son of Aegeus!
> But all this you know without my telling you.
> Now to that spot. The god within me calls.[13]

The life of Oedipus, as it is revealed in these two plays, parallels the alchemical process. Like the *prima materia* with which the alchemists began their work, Oedipus is subjected to fiery ordeals and sufferings until he is transformed into a holy object that benefits all who touch him. Here is the *theophany* that redeems the suffering of the first play.

Taken together, the two Oedipus plays reveal explicitly the four stages of Greek tragedy. The *agon* is represented by Oedipus' encounter with the Sphinx, followed later by the struggle to discover the hidden crime that was causing the plague; the *pathos* comes with the blinding insight and the ego defeat that it caused; the *threnos* is expressed by the chorus, which bemoans the downfall of the mighty Oedipus, and by Oedipus' prolonged wanderings; and the *theophany* arrives at the end of *Oedipus at Colonus,* when his tomb becomes a sacred sanctuary and a perpetual blessing. These four stages portray quite precisely the steps in every major increase of consciousness. In each case a suffering, deflating ordeal for the ego must precede the epiphany of the Self. This is necessary because the ego starts out in a state of identification with the Self. It can only realize its separate and dependent condition by a tragic ordeal that enforces the separation. Sophocles describes this process in the final lines of *Antigone:*

Where wisdom is, there happiness will crown
A piety that nothing will corrode.
But high and mighty words and ways
Are flogged to humbleness, till age,
Beaten to its knees, at last is wise.[14]

9

Shrines and Oracles

THE SHRINES and oracles of ancient Greece, according to the literature that has been preserved, played a large role in the thinking of the ancients. Whenever one speaks of oracles, the Delphic oracle, the most famous one, comes to mind. It was believed to be the center of the universe, marked by a huge stone called the omphalos; by going to the center, one's questions could be answered. A priestess was consulted who is said to have sat over a cleft in the earth that descended into the depths and out of which vapors arose. She would inhale the vapors and go into a trance and then pronounce the oracle or the answer to the question, a precise analogy of our consulting the images that arise from the unconscious. The long pilgrimage required to visit the oracle, sometimes from as far away as Asia Minor, indicates that great import was attached to the enterprise.

Evidently the replies received were often ambiguous, allowing for an experience such as takes place today when one consults the *I Ching,* the Chinese oracle book, where one projects into the ambiguous answer one's own unconscious wisdom, so to speak. A classic example of that ambiguity was the answer Croesus, the king of

Lydia, received from the Delphic oracle. Yearning to invade Persia, he consulted the oracle about his prospects and was told that if Croesus attacked the Persians, he would destroy a great empire. Elated by the response, he launched his campaign, only to discover that the great empire to be destroyed was his own. The story suggests the risk in consulting the unconscious for the ego's advantage.

A second important pilgrimage was associated with the shrines of Asclepius; the two most significant ones were located on the island of Kos and at Epidaurus. Asclepius was the child of Apollo and Coronis, but Coronis proved unfaithful to her divine lover and was killed. Asclepius was then rescued and raised by the centaur Cheiron, who was responsible for all his healing knowledge. Cheiron, who had been injured by Heracles' arrows and suffered from an unhealing wound, stands for the wounded healer, the one who can cure others despite and because of his own suffering. Another expression of this paradoxical image is the myth that Asclepius received his healing potions or powers from Athena, who gave him the blood of Medusa. According to the story, there were two vials of that blood, one taken from Medusa's right side and the other from the left. The first was immensely healing in its powers and could even raise the dead, but the blood from the left side was instantly destructive. We have a residue of that paradoxical imagery in the two snakes that are wound around the winged staff of Hermes in the caduceus, the symbol of the medical profession. According to ancient belief, one of those snakes was poisonous and the other healing, as if one ejected blood from the left side of Medusa and the other from the right. This elemental idea appears in different symbolic images, but the basic notion remains the same, namely, that the unconscious has a double quality to it. One can never know in advance whether it will be beneficial or harmful, since this depends on the circumstances and also on the attitude of the ego that is relating to the unconscious power.

A procedure prevalent at the shrines of Asclepius is described in some detail in C. A. Meier's book *Ancient Incubation and Modern Psychotherapy*.[1] If one were ill and a cure did not promptly come, one considered making a pilgrimage to the shrine of the temple of Asclepius. (Here again, we must take into account the importance that was projected into the visit and the great effort of making the trip, which would affect the dynamics of what happened.) Once the patient arrived at the temple, certain purification ceremonies and bathings would be undergone. According to some sources, there were entrance requirements, partially having to do with one's moral character. Once these were passed, the patient would sleep in the sanctuary, where he would have a dream that would bring the healing. It was often thought that a god would come in the dream and touch the wounded or sick spot to heal it with his touch. This can be recognized as a precursor of our current thinking about the nature of the unconscious and the potential healing value of consulting it. Apparently, following the healing dream, the patient was required to relate it and discuss it with the priest of the temple, prefiguring the psychotherapeutic process.

One of the notable features of the Asclepian myth is that curing someone who was meant to die would lead to the healer's own death in place of the one cured. In fact that became Asclepius' fate. He had brought Hippolytus back to life through his healing power, but this

FIG. 23. Ascelpius appears to a sick man. (Transcription by J. Wheelock after a votive relief, now lost.)

transcended what was meant to be and thus Asclepius himself was killed by Zeus for challenging divine decree. We are reminded of how literal such psychological images can be by an experience that Jung describes as occurring to him when he almost died following a heart attack. He tells in his memoirs of having left the earth and viewed some remarkable things high above the world and was quite caught up with the ecstatic quality of what he was experiencing when

From below, from the direction of Europe, an image floated up. It was my doctor, Doctor H.—or rather, his likeness—framed by a golden chain or a golden laurel wreath. I knew at once: "Aha, this is my doctor, of course, the one who has been treating me. But now he is coming in his primal form, as a *basileus* of Kos [a prince of Kos, where the sanctuary of Asclepius was; so it was in his Asclepian form that his doctor was coming]. In life he was an avatar of this *basileus,* the temporal embodiment of the primal form, which has existed from the beginning. Now he is appearing in that primal form."

Presumably I too was in my primal form, though this was something I did not observe, but simply took for granted. As he stood before me, a mute exchange of thought took place between us. Dr. H. had been delegated by the earth to deliver a message to me, to tell me that there was a protest against my going away. I had no right to leave the earth and must return. The moment I heard that, the vision ceased.

I was profoundly disappointed, for now it all seemed to have been for nothing. The painful process of defoliation had been in vain, and I was not allowed to [proceed].

. . . I felt violent resistance to my doctor because he had brought me back to life. At the same time, I was worried about him. "His life is in danger, for heaven's sake! He has appeared to me in his primal form! When anybody attains this form it means he is going to die, for already he belongs to the 'greater company'!" Suddenly the terrifying thought came to me that Dr. H. would have to die in my stead. I tried my best to talk to him about it, but he did not understand me. Then I became angry with him. "Why does he always pretend he doesn't know he is a *basileus* of Kos? And that he has already assumed his primal form? He wants to make me believe that he doesn't know!" That irritated me. My wife reproved me for being so unfriendly to him. She was right; but at the time I was angry with him for stubbornly refusing to speak of all that had passed between us in my vision. "Damn it all, he ought to watch his step. He has no right to be so reckless! I want to tell him to take care of himself." I was firmly convinced that his life was in jeopardy.

In actual fact I was his last patient. On April 4, 1944—I still remember the exact date—I was allowed to sit up on the edge of my bed for the first time since the beginning of my illness, and on this same day, Dr. H. took to his bed and did not leave it again.[2]

So these images that are enshrined in myth, when encountered at a certain level of psychic experience (which, of course, is rare), are demonstrated to possess some kind of objective reality.

In addition to Delphi, Kos, and Epidaurus, we learn from the ancient writers about a shrine known as the oracle of Trophonius, an oracle apparently consulted in the main by those seeking visionary experience. The oracle of Trophonius was a cave oracle, and after suitable preparation the prospective seeker descended into the cave through a narrow cleft just wide enough for the body, and remained there until an answer came, either as an auditory response or as a visual one. Fortunately an account survives of an individual, Timarchus, who consulted the oracle of Trophonius and gave a detailed description of his experience. Although this account may very well have received literary embellishment, there are reasons to believe that at least originally, it derived from an actual experience, one reason being that the individual leaves the earth and floats off in a way that parallels certain known visions, such as the one Jung had when he came close to death. This is how the story is recounted by Plutarch:

> [Timarchus descends into the crypt of Trophonius, first performing the rites that are customary at the oracle.] He remained underground two nights and a day, and most people had already given up hope, and his family were lamenting him for dead, when he came up in the morning with a radiant countenance. . . . [He] began to tell us of the many wonders seen and heard.

The vision he then describes can be understood as a revelation of the structure of the psyche, rather than of the structure of the universe or of life after death. A psychological approach to such material as this gives us a view of the psyche itself in a way not ordinarily seen.

> He said that on descending into the oracular crypt his first experience was of profound darkness; next, after a prayer, he lay a long time not clearly aware whether he was awake or dreaming. It did seem to him, however, that at the same moment he heard a crash and was struck on the head, and that the sutures parted and released his soul. As it withdrew and mingled joyfully with air that was translucent and pure, it felt in the first place that now, after long being cramped, it had again found relief, and was growing larger than before, spreading out like a sail; and next that it faintly caught the whir of something revolving overhead with a pleasant sound [the same sort of experiences that Jung had]. When he lifted his eyes the earth was nowhere to be seen; but he saw islands illuminated by one another with soft fire, taking on now one color, now another, like a dye, as the light kept varying with their mutations. They appeared countless in number and huge in size, and though not all equal, yet all alike round; and he fancied that their circular movement made a musical whirring in the aether, for the gentleness of the sound resulting from the harmony of all the separate sounds corresponded to the evenness of their motion.

A noteworthy aspect of the vision is the iridescent play of many colors that he experienced in the spherical islands, an image familiar from alchemical symbolism, where the peacock's tail and its play and display of many colors expresses the emergence of the Self, the totality. The musical whirring refers to the music of the spheres, which was a characteristic feature of ancient thought, and the vision also emphasizes the movement of the spheres, floating islands that were revolving along a circular pathway. So we have repeated images of roundness and the circle, which Jung has shown to be aspects of totality symbolism. These spherical islands did not turn in actual circles, but rather in a spiral motion, indicating that they combined two different motions, the circular and the linear, and this is just the characteristic image of development, which proceeds around and around the center of the psyche but at the same time also follows a developmental pathway toward an end.

Timarchus eventually carried on a dialogue with a voice, which asked if he wanted anything explained, and he characteristically replied: "Yes, everything!" The voice said:

> The turning point of birth is at the moon. For while the rest of the islands belong to the gods, the moon belongs to terrestrial daemons and avoids the Styx by passing slightly above it; [however, the earth and the river Styx occasionally catch it and then, when they do] as the Styx draws near the souls cry out in terror for many slip off and are carried away by Hades; others, whose cessation of birth falls out at the proper moment, swim up from below and are rescued by the moon. . . .[3]

Here we see that souls descending from the heavenly regions to be born on earth pass by the moon, and souls that are leaving their earthly abode and going back to heaven do also. The moon is the gateway, so to speak, between heaven and earth. Jung discusses this image in *Mysterium Coniunctionis:*

> According to the ancient view, the moon stands on the border-line between the eternal, aethereal things and the ephemeral phenomena of the earthly, sublunar realm. Macrobius [an ancient writer] says: "The realm of the perishable begins with the moon and goes downwards. Souls coming into this region begin to be subject to the numbering of days and to time. . . . There is no doubt that the moon is the author and contriver of mortal bodies."[4]

Thus we have the idea that the principle the moon signifies stands between the ego and the transpersonal psyche; the moon is the gateway or transition between those two. That is simply the ancient symbolic way of saying what Jung has formulated more precisely, at least for a man's psyche, by saying that the anima is the gateway to the unconscious. It is via the feminine principle and the powers of embodiment it signifies that the moon brings things into conscious realization and withdraws them from conscious realization. Timarchus goes on to say that he does not see these souls going back and forth from the moon. He says:

[All I see are] many stars trembling about the abyss, others sinking into it, and others again shooting up from below.

"Then without knowing it," the being replies, "you see the daemons* themselves. Every soul partakes of understanding, none is irrational or unintelligent. But the portion of the soul that mingles with flesh and passions suffers alteration and becomes in the pleasures and pains it undergoes irrational. Not every soul mingles to the same extent; some sink entirely into the body . . . others mingle in part, but leave outside what is purest in them. . . . Thus, Timarchus," [he says], "in the stars that are apparently extinguished, you must understand that you see the souls that sink entirely into the body; in the stars that are lighted again, as it were, and reappear from below, you must understand that you see the souls that float back from the body after death, shaking off a sort of dimness and darkness as one might shake off mud; while the stars that move about on high are the daemons of men such as possess understanding."[5]

We find this image of the stars sinking into the darkness of matter and then reemerging out of it again in other notions of light or fire that descend from heaven into the darkness of matter. In Gnosticism, for instance, it is Sophia, the light that falls into the embrace of dark matter and then must be redeemed from that condition. Or in the late Cabbalah of Isaac Luria there is the image of the primal light that was poured into vessels, but the vessels broke and the light spilled out into the darkness and now has to be collected again. It is an image of consciousness temporarily lost or hidden in the unconscious, waiting to be redeemed and recollected, much like the little droplets of mercury that can be reassembled and brought back into one large drop, which fascinated the alchemists so much.

---

*This ancient meaning of the word *daemon* refers to the spiritual essence of the person, not to the negative aspect that has later been attached to the word *demon*.

Dionysus

THE STORY of Dionysus' beginnings is remarkable for his difficulty
in coming into the world. Conceived in the union of Zeus and the
mortal woman Semele, he fell victim to jealous Hera even before he
was born. Knowing what the consequences of her advice would be,
Hera persuaded Semele, who was already six months pregnant, to
insist that her mysterious lover reveal himself to her in his true form.
When she did so, she was destroyed by the sight of Zeus in his full
power. "It is a terrible thing to fall into the hands of the living god."[1]
Zeus plucked the unborn child from Semele's body and sewed him
up in his thigh, where Dionysus spent the three remaining months.
Shortly following his birth as a horned infant crowned with serpents,
and again at the instigation of Hera, he was torn to pieces by the
Titans from which he derived the name Zagreus, meaning approximately "dismembered." His body was then consumed by the Titans
except for his heart, which was recovered and from which he was
reconstituted and reborn. Entrusted finally to the charge of Persephone, he was more protected and in fact grew up in various situations in the company of protective women and nymphs. As an adult,
he was described as somewhat feminine in appearance and he went
always in the company of groups of Maenads (the word means "mad
women") who had become his devotees.

FIG. 24. Dionysus bearing ivy sprays and a drinking horn. (Detail of an Attic cup, c. 500 BC. Hermitage Museum, St. Petersburg.)

Dionysus was a wanderer, traveling through the world with the bands of Maenads, setting up his worship and bringing the culture of grapes and wine. He is pictured as a beautiful young man draped in a fawn skin, holding the thyrsus, a staff or wand made of a fennel stalk wound with ivy. His rituals were held in the woods, in uncivilized nature. He was associated with the bull and with serpents, the imagery pointing to his wildness and his power, and to his place outside the bounds of civilized order. Thought of as "the God who comes," he would appear unexpectedly in a new place, bringing excitement, joy, and terror, and changing what was there before.

The classic account of Dionysus is to be found in Euripides' *The Bacchae*. In this play, he comes to Thebes and what he brings with him destroys the status quo. When King Pentheus of Thebes returned to his kingdom to find that Dionysus and his followers were holding ecstatic celebrations in the woods and that many of the local people, especially the women, were joining them, he was outraged and vowed to lock up the revelers and punish Dionysus. The authority or power principle stiffens and becomes vengeful in the face of Dionysian wildness. When Dionysus appeared to him, Pentheus defied the wild god and tried to lock him up, but after the king had him bound with knotted ropes and deposited in his stables, a bull was discovered in his place. Dionysus had slipped through his fingers. Pentheus gradually turned mad himself, under the influence of the appearing and disappearing god, finally attempting to spy on the Bacchic revelers in the woods, where he was discovered and torn to pieces by the crazed devotees, who included his own mother. Two old wise men of the city, Teiresias, the blind seer, and Cadmus, the former king, decided, as aged as they were, to join the celebrations in the woods; they knew that everyone must honor Dionysus and could feel the invigorating power of his presence. Teiresias says:

> . . . this god is a prophet; the Bacchic ecstasy
> And frenzy hold a strong prophetic element.
> When he fills irresistibly a human body
> He gives those so possessed power to foretell the future.[2]

The two old men returned safely from the revels, but not so the king who had refused to honor Dionysus—one need not become possessed by the god, only respectfully acknowledge him, perhaps risking one's dignity.

What Dionysus brings is wild, spontaneous, inspired behavior. If Apollo signifies measure and mean, Dionysus symbolizes excess and the value and significance of excess. There is ecstasy on the one hand and terror on the other, and the whole potential for inner transformation. He is connected to rapture, to the release of everything that has been locked up, to the blaze of life, but also to persecution, suffering, and death, and to madness. He is associated with Persephone, the queen of the Underworld. He brings wisdom in a sudden flash, epiphany, and also the suddenly recognized truth that can lead to madness. Where he is, things change.

What actually occurred in the Dionysian rites is not altogether known, but a certain amount of information is accumulated in Jane Harrison's book *Prolegomena to the Study of Greek Religion.* She describes, for instance, the rite of omophagia, the ritual eating of raw flesh, which is alluded to in a fragment of a lost play of Euripides, where this is written:

> Where midnight Zagreus roves, I rove;
> I have endured his thunder-cry;
> Fulfilled his red and bleeding feasts;
> Held the Great Mother's mountain flame;
> I am Set Free and named by name
> A Bacchos of the Mailed Priests.[3]

Clement of Alexandria also refers to this rite of the raw flesh. He says this:

> The Bacchoi hold orgies in honor of a mad Dionysus, they celebrate a divine madness by the Eating of Raw Flesh, the final accomplishment of their rite is the distribution of the flesh of butchered victims, they are crowned with snakes, and shriek out the name of Eva . . . and the symbol of their Bacchic orgies is a consecrated serpent.[4]

Usually a bull or a goat representing the god was dismembered in a ritual reenactment of the dismemberment of the infant Dionysus, and the raw and bleeding flesh was then distributed and eaten by all the participants, who thus took on the role of the Titans.

In punishment for the Titans' dismemberment of Dionysus, Zeus had hurled a thunderbolt at them, which had reduced them to dust, but that dust had little sparks of Dionysus scattered in it because they had all eaten him, and that Titan dust was later used to make human beings. Hence, we are made out of Titan dust with the Dionysian spark in us that is left over from the Titans' meal. Such was the mythical story the omophagian rite reenacted.

What would such a rite represent psychologically? It certainly echoes totem meals that we know of in various societies, and it is a remarkable, if crude, parallel to the Christian Eucharist. If the Dionysian principle can be thought of as a primordial dynamism, the experience of dismemberment would correspond to a voluntary breaking up of elemental psychic or spiritual energy, to make it available for the emerging conscious ego. There are subtle and profound ideas implied in the image.

The dismemberment of Dionysus was the subject of much theological speculation by the Neoplatonists. Proclus, one of their most prolific writers, spoke about the symbolic meaning of the fact that the infant Dionysus was playing with a mirror at the time he was seized by the Titans and dismembered. Proclus saw this as indicating that the heavenly Dionysus caught sight of his image in the mirror of matter, went forth toward it with desire, and was thus confined in matter, incarnated.[5] He became a divisible soul, one made of separate parts or personalities and thus was subject to dismemberment by the Titans. We are confronted here with the complicated problem that has occupied philosophers since the beginning of human thought, the problem of unity versus multiplicity. Proclus expressed the idea that Dionysus represented original unity, which sees its image in the mirror of matter, and, out of the desire to be incarnated or to be born into real spatio-temporal existence, submits itself to multiplicity, to being broken up into specific parts in time and space. Psychologically, this refers to becoming an ego. To the extent that egohood is born, one becomes a multiplicity, since one must pay attention to concrete reality, which is not a unity, but a multiplicity. The conflicting demands that result tear us apart in different directions. Life in the flesh is multiple; singleness belongs in the transcendental realm.

The well-known verses of Shelley allude to this same problem. These are from his poem "Adonais":

The One remains, the many change and pass;
Heaven's light forever shines, Earth's shadows fly;
Life, like a dome of many-coloured glass,
Stains the white radiance of Eternity, . . .[6]

We could say that Dionysus is the white radiance of eternity that voluntarily submits to dismemberment, fragmentation, refraction into specific colors in order to generate the particular colors of light and of actual existence, rather than just remaining eternal white unity.

The ritual of the feast of the raw flesh, at the same time, bears a close relationship with Communion symbolism. As reenacted in the Mass, Christ experienced sacrifice and dismemberment in order that he become food for the believers, just as Dionysus in the guise of the animal served that function in the more primitive rite. Dionysus suffered incarnation and dismemberment just as Christ suffered it with the Crucifixion and with the symbolic dismemberment of the Last Supper, at which he breaks the bread he calls his body. In a medieval woodcut of the Crucifixion reproduced in Alan Watts's book, *Myth and Ritual in Christianity,* dismembered arms and legs are shown hanging on the cross, indicating that these two images, crucifixion and dismemberment, can be equated.[7] It seems that the divinity, or the archetypal psyche, permits itself to become manifest and endures fragmentation in order to promote life. This dream of a young man alludes to that point:

> I dreamed that I saw a modern Christ figure who was traveling in a bus with a group of disciples. Then I sensed that there was danger. The man was going to be betrayed. It happened and the bus rocked with violence. The figure was set upon and subdued. They had apparently tied ropes to each of his hands and feet and had pulled him tight, spread-eagled in four directions. I knew they would kill him that way. [There was going to be a quartering, a dismemberment.] Then it appeared, when I looked at him more closely, that he was not tied by the hands, but was grasping with each hand a wooden bar attached to the rope. He was cooperating in his own death. At the end of the dream came an image of a magnetic field of force showing the forces pulling him apart in the four directions, making a cross with the field of force between the four poles.

Here is a dream of dismemberment, which is clearly a profound process, as well as a sacred one since it is associated with religious ritual. It should be noted that the archetype or the deity itself is subject to this dismemberment, not the ego.

Creativity is an aspect of Dionysus, and one of particular psychological importance. It is not a deliberate Hephaestian creativity, but creativity in the inspired, almost intoxicated, sense, in which the unconscious wells up. It corresponds to the way Nietzsche said he wrote *Thus Spake Zarathustra;* while he tramped the mountains of the Engadine, Zarathustra shouted in his ear. That is Dionysus, that is Dionysian creativity, and Nietzsche is probably the outstanding example of Dionysian possession. Following his mental breakdown, at times he signed himself "Crucified," at times "Dionysus," at times "Zagreus," showing how close certain aspects of the myth of Christ are to the myth of Dionysus. Jung has written on the subject of identification with the creative principle in his seminar on Nietzsche's *Zarathustra.* He talks about the creative powers as they manifested themselves in Nietzsche:

[The creative forces] have you on the string and you dance to their whistling, to their melody. But inasmuch as you say that these creative forces are in Nietzsche or in me or anywhere else, you cause an inflation, because man does not possess creative powers, he is possessed by them. . . . If he allows himself to be thoroughly possessed by them without questioning, without looking at them, there is no inflation, but the moment he splits off, when he thinks "I am the fellow" an inflation follows. . . . [It can only be avoided] by obeying completely without attempting to look at yourself. You must be quite naive. [But] It happens automatically that you become conscious of yourself and then you are gone; it is as if you had touched a high-tension wire. . . . Nietzsche of course could not help looking at the thing and then he was overwhelmed with resentments, because the creative powers steal your time, sap your strength, and what is the result? A book perhaps. But where is your personal life? All gone. Therefore, such people feel so terribly cheated; they mind it, and everybody ought to kneel down before them in order to make up for that which has been stolen by God. . . . If you know you are creative and enjoy being creative, you will be crucified afterwards, because anybody identified with God will be dismembered. An old father of the church, the Bishop Synesius said that the *spiritus phantasticus,* man's creative spirit, can penetrate the depths or the heights of the universe like God or like a great demon, but on account of that, he will also have to undergo the divine punishment. That would be the dismemberment of Dionysus or the crucifixion of Christ.[8]

So people who are intoxicated by some creative effort should be warned that the only safe creativity is that which makes one uncomfortable. If one feels burdened down with every sentence one writes or every brush stroke comes with an effort, then one is safe and not in danger of falling, one is already down. But otherwise, to identify with Dionysus has the opposite danger, and Nietzsche is an appalling example of this.

These reflections help us to understand the psychological effect of communion symbolism, whether it be the rite of the raw flesh in more primitive times or the modern Christian communion. One effect of participating in the ritual would be to spare the participant the fate of God. It protects one from identification with the inner creative powers, since by acting out the role of the communicant, the receiver of the divine nourishment, one is taking on a humble position and is thus protected against inflation.

The central symbol of Dionysus is the grape, the product of which is wine and the essence of which is alcohol. Early man was profoundly impressed by the effects of alcohol. It is indeed a mysterious and miraculous substance, which when drunk, changes the personality; it has a true power of transformation that led early people to believe that wine contained a spirit. This is why alcoholic beverages are still called "spirits" and why the Latin name for whiskey is *spiritus frumenti,* the spirit of the grain. This remarkable substance lends itself to the projection of profound psychological imagery and Dionysus is the name of the mysterious transforming spirit that is symbolized by its effects. By extension, it is the principle of creativity, life renewal, and the unpredictable qualities of the spirit as such, the spirit that blows where it will. In this symbolic sense, the verses of Omar Khayyam's *Rubaiyat* become a hymn not to banal, vulgar alcohol but to the spirit of Dionysus and what that represents psychologically. For example:

You know, my Friends, how long since in my House
For a new Marriage I did make Carouse:

Divorced old barren Reason from my Bed,
And took the Daughter of the Vine to Spouse.

And:

The Grape that can with Logic absolute
The Two-and-Seventy jarring Sects confute;
The subtle Alchemist that in a Trice
Life's leaden Metal into Gold transmute.[9]

Here wine, along with what it symbolizes, is equated with the *elixir vitae* or *aqua permanens* of the alchemist.* In Christian psychology, the Dionysian principle was largely relegated to the devil and so lived, at least in part, an underground existence. But we see Dionysus as he was starting to emerge in the modern mind in John Milton's poem "Comus." Identified by Milton as the son of Circe and Dionysus, Comus is pictured as a kind of degraded Dionysian figure, who lived in a dark wood where he accosted travelers and offered them his wine in a crystal goblet. The effect of the wine was to turn them partly into beasts. Here is Milton's description:

[He] excels his mother [Circe] at her mighty art,
Offering to every weary traveller
His orient liquor in a crystal glass,
To quench the drouth of Phoebus; which, as they taste
(For most do taste through fond intemperate thirst),
Soon as the potion works, their human countenance,
The express resemblance of the gods, is changed
Into some brutish form of wolf, or bear,
Or ounce, or tiger, hog, or bearded goat,
All other parts remaining as they were;
And they, so perfect is their misery,
Not once perceive their foul disfigurement,
But boast themselves more comely than before;

*This imagery is further developed in my book *Ego and Archetype*, pp. 235ff.

And all their friends and native home forget,
To roll with pleasure in a sensual sty.[10]

The unconscious in its spontaneous aspect still has here a largely
negative cast. However, something new is introduced when a chaste
lady gets lost in Comus' woods, is rescued barely in time, and fails to
succumb to his temptation. Then the poet reveals that he speaks for
an age of transition, because although his Comus is still evil, Milton
puts the best lines in Comus' mouth, prompting William Blake to say
about Milton in *The Marriage of Heaven and Hell:* "The reason Milton wrote in fetters when he wrote of Angels and God, and at liberty
when of Devils and Hell, is that he was a true Poet and of the Devil's
party without knowing it."[11]

Although the chaste lady refuses Comus' wine, he replies to her:

Oh, foolishness of men! That lend their ears
To those budge doctors of the Stoic fur,
And fetch their precepts from the Cynic tub,
Praising the lean and sallow abstinence.
Wherefore did Nature pour her bounties forth
With such a full and unwithdrawing hand,
Covering the earth with odours, fruits, and flocks,
Thronging the seas with spawn innumerable,
But all to please and sate the curious taste?
And set to work millions of spinning worms,
That in their green shops weave the smooth-haired silk
To deck her sons; and that no corner might
Be vacant of her plenty, in her own loins
She hutched the all-worshipped ore, and precious gems
To store her children with: if all the world
Should in a pet of temperance feed on pulse,
Drink the clear stream, and nothing wear but frieze,
The All-giver would be unthanked, would be unpraised,
Not half his riches known, and yet despised;
And we should serve him as a grudging master,
As a penurious niggard of his wealth,

And live like Nature's bastards, not her sons,
Who would be quite surcharged with her own weight
And strangled with her waste fertility;
The earth cumbered and the winged air darked with plumes,
The herds would over-multitude their lords,
The sea o'er fraught would swell, and the unsought diamonds
Would so emblaze the forehead of the deep
And so bestud with stars, that they below
Would grow inured to light, and come at last
To gaze upon the sun with shameless brows.

Getting back to the point, he says:

List, lady, be not coy and be not cozened
With that same vaunted name, virginity.
Beauty is Nature's coin, must not be hoarded. . . .[12]

Milton is thus expressing the intriguing idea that to spurn the Dionysian wine and not to avail ourselves of what nature has to offer con-
stitutes *hybris,* because it means that all the diamonds of the deep
then go uncollected, so to speak, and the deep can't tell itself apart
from the sky.

The appearance of the Dionysian principle in dreams is not uncommon and some of the most powerful Dionysian dreams are
dreamt by clergymen, which, given the law of opposites, is not surprising: those most affected by the repression of the Dionysian principle would be just the ones whose unconscious could be expected to
present it in most vivid form. For example, Jung, in *Psychology and
Alchemy,* tells of a clergyman dreaming that on entering his church
one night, he found that the whole wall of the choir has collapsed.
The altar and ruins are overgrown with vines hanging full of grapes
and the moon is shining in through the gap.[13]

Here is another Dionysian dream in abbreviated form:

I am to celebrate communion. In the sacristy, which looks like a
kitchen, the communion wine is to be prepared by mixing two separate

wines, a dark blue wine and a red wine. The latter is in a bottle with a yellow label that looks like a Scotch label and is marked "Paul." Two men are sitting at a round table. One is a political leftist, the other a rightist. Up to now they have maintained a facade of social amenity, but now they are becoming hostile to one another. I suggest that they ventilate their reactions and resolve their feeling relationship. At this point, the scene darkens as in a theater play and a red-yellow spotlight focuses on a small table between and behind the two men. On the table is a bottle of the warm red wine with the Scotch label clearly marked "Paul." Then there is total darkness and the tinkle of glasses sounding as though they have been clinked and perhaps broken. The sense is obvious in the dream. I think, they've drunk the red wine in their discussion attaining comradeship, become drunk in the process, fallen asleep and dropped their glasses. My response is delight in the aesthetic way in which this has been portrayed and anxiety about the fact that the service needs to begin and we do not now have the ingredients for the communion wine.

One might think of the two kinds of wine, a blue wine and a red, as signifying the spirit of Logos, or heaven, on one hand, and the spirit of earth, or Eros, on the other. The impression is given that there are two different degrees of reconciliation to be achieved and the higher degree would be the communion service with the mixed wine, which is not reached yet. A lesser union takes place first, the union of opposites of the two men, the rightist and the leftist, through their getting drunk on the red wine. This corresponds to a kind of reconciliation with the shadow, or a union of opposites on the shadow level; the anima component is not present. Demonstrating an important aspect of Dionysian symbolism, this particular image tells us that Dionysus and what he signifies promotes a sense of communion with humanity and a dissolution of differences—a quality of the Dionysian that has been expressed by Nietzsche in a passage from his essay *The Birth of Tragedy:*

Under the charm of the Dionysian not only is the union between man and man reaffirmed, but nature which has become alienated, hostile or subjugated, celebrates once more her reconciliation with her lost son, man. Freely, earth proffers her gifts and peacefully the beasts of prey of the rocks and desert approach. The chariot of Dionysus is covered with flowers and garlands; panthers and tigers walk under its yoke. Transform Beethoven's "Hymn to Joy" into a painting; let your imagination conceive the multitudes bowing to the dust, awestruck—then you will approach the Dionysian. Now the slave is a free man; now all the rigid, hostile barriers that necessity, caprice or "impudent convention" have fixed between man and man, are broken. Now with the gospel of universal harmony, each one feels himself not only united, reconciled and fused with his neighbor, but as one with him, as if the veil of *maya* had been torn aside, and were now merely fluttering in tatters before the mysterious primordial unity.[14]

The Dionysian effect of dissolving all differences and promoting the primordial unity is likewise an attribute of the blood of Christ, according to Paul. Take, for instance, this passage:

But now in Christ Jesus you who once were far off have been brought near in the blood of Christ. For he is our peace, who has made us both one, and has broken down the dividing wall of hostility, by abolishing in his flesh the law of commandments and ordinances, that he might create in himself one new man in place of the two, so making peace and might reconcile us both to God in one body through the cross, thereby bringing the hostility to an end.[15]

What is spoken of by Paul is precisely the effect that the red wine labeled "Paul" had in the dream. However, there are two ways of taking this breakdown of all dividing lines and reconciliation of all differences and return to primordial unity. Taken purely externally it can amount to a regression to unconscious collective identification and the phenomenon of mob psychology. But taken as referring to an inner process, it signifies the unification and harmonizing of the individual personality.

Certainly the wine of Dionysus symbolizes a powerful but paradoxical content, like the spirit Mercurius in alchemical symbolism, which is poisonous to some at certain times and healing to others at other times. Not for nothing did Christianity relegate Dionysus to the devil. However, when his time has come, when he is truly knocking on the gates of one's city of Thebes, then to deny the Dionysian principle is a grave mistake, although to embrace it superficially and frivolously can also be unwise—a fact strikingly indicated by the symbolic implications of Paul's statement in First Corinthians, in which he says:

> . . . anyone who eats the bread or drinks the cup of the Lord unworthily will be guilty of desecrating the body and blood of the Lord. A man must test himself before eating his share of the bread and drinking from the cup. For he who eats and drinks eats and drinks judgment on himself if he does not discern the Body.[16]

"The Body" here refers to discerning the deity he is incorporating, with the realization that there is indeed a sacred nature. Only with that awareness can the creativity and spontaneity of the psyche be realized without either an infantile regression or a presumptuous inflation. To return to the words of Euripides, we could say as Dionysus says in the *The Bacchae*, "[I come] establishing my mysteries and rites that I might be revealed on earth for what I am, a god."[17]

Orphism

WHAT WE call Orphism or the Orphic religion is generally acknowledged as the highest religious manifestation of the ancient world, deriving originally from the simple myth of Orpheus, the miraculous musician. It was a spiritualization of the original Dionysian rituals, which were of a much cruder nature. Orphism underlay a good bit of Greek philosophy. Plato cast into philosophical form many Orphic doctrines and in places in Plato's works the recasting is made explicit. Certain brotherhoods, such as the Pythagoreans, probably had an Orphic basis. Also, many aspects of Orphism had remarkable analogies to what later became Christian doctrine.

The basic material of Orphism is found in the myth of Orpheus, which later became elaborated in more religious terms. Orpheus' playing of the lyre was said to be so enchanting he could charm wild beasts into serenity and even make trees and rocks move and follow his melodies. In short, his music was utterly irresistible, and it is a striking metaphor of the power of civilizing consciousness. The central story is that Orpheus' wife, Eurydice, was killed by a snake bite while fleeing the erotic advances of Aristaeus—she was a victim, that is, of primitive instinctual energies. Orpheus was overcome with despair at her loss and he descended to the Underworld to retrieve her. Through the powers of his music he charmed the hell-dog Cerberus

FIG. 25. Orpheus plays his lyre for a bemused audience. (Detail of an Attic krater, c. 430 BC. Staatliche Museen zu Berlin—Preussischer Kulturbesitz.)

and even temporarily suspended the tortures of the damned. He convinced Hades to let him take Eurydice back, with the important proviso that he must not look back at Eurydice, who would be following him, until they were both fully in the upper world. He did not quite manage it; he looked too soon and Eurydice was snatched back to the Underworld. Accounts vary as to what followed, but for one reason or another Orpheus was dismembered, apparently by a band of Maenads, and his head was thrown into a river where it continued to sing. It floated down the stream and landed on the Isle of Lesbos, where it became an oracular shrine.

The stories differ as to just why the dismemberment occurred. One story recounts that Orpheus served Apollo and neglected Dionysus and was dismembered for that reason. Other stories tell us that he was indeed a priest of Dionysus and in his priesthood grew into such a state of identification with the god that he suffered Dionysus' fate of dismemberment. Thus at the very beginning an overlap of the image of Orpheus with the image of Dionysus appears that continued later in the cult that developed as Orphism. Precisely what belonged to Orpheus cannot be determined.

At the most basic psychological level, this myth pictures the loss of the anima to the unconscious and a noble effort to retrieve her that does not quite succeed. However, the religion that crystallized around the figure of Orpheus did so for a different reason, which was that Orpheus had made the journey of the *nekyia,* the trip to the Underworld, and had returned with the transcendent knowledge that is to be derived from the depths.

The Orphics were concerned with the art of living. They were strict vegetarians and highly ascetic; they concentrated on how one should live in order to be rewarded after death. The reward would come to the one who lived his life correctly, and punishment at death to the one who had lived wrongly. This is an example of what is widespread in religious thinking—the projection of the goal of individuation onto the afterlife. This is set forth in books of the dead and in various instructions as to how the dead person should proceed, which in a sense constitute manuals of individuation.

Along with this aspect of the Orphic doctrine came a concern with keeping oneself pure as part of the ascetic ideal. Much influenced by Orphic doctrines, Plato could be considered a philosophic Orphic. In the *Phaedo* Socrates says this about philosophic purification from pleasures and fears:

> Truth is in fact a purification from all these things, and self-restraint and justice and courage and wisdom itself are a kind of purification. And I fancy that those men who established the mysteries [Orphic mysteries] were not unenlightened, but in reality had a hidden meaning when they said long ago that whoever goes uninitiated and unsanctified to the other world will lie in the mire, but he who arrives there initiated and purified will dwell with the Gods. For as they say in the mysteries, "the thyrsus bearers[1] are many, but the mystics few;" and these mystics are, I believe, those who have been true philosophers. And I in my life have, so far as I could, left nothing undone, and have striven in every way to make myself one of them. But whether I have

striven aright and have met with success, I believe I shall know clearly, when I have arrived there, very soon, if it is God's will.[2]

This is pure Orphism translated into philosophic terms. Those he calls the initiated and purified philosophers are, in psychological terms, those who have submitted to the rigors of the individuation process. The mire that the uninitiated fall into represents the mud of the unconscious that has not been worked on psychologically, that is, the *prima materia* that has not undergone development.

As it had been in ancient Egypt, the goal of right living was projected into the afterlife among the Orphics. Certain instructions for finding their way after death were buried with members of the Orphic community when they died. Some of these tombs from about the third century BC have been discovered, and fortunately the instructions were engraved on imperishable gold tablets, indicating how important they must have been considered. Containing in concise, abbreviated form directions for the soul on how to proceed in the afterworld, they are similar to the instructions in the Egyptian *Book of the Dead,* and in all cases these directions can be thought of as symbolic expressions of how to reach the goal of individuation. Since nobody knows what does happen in the afterlife, the instructions become a kind of projection screen for unconscious contents to express themselves.

The Orphic tablets are not all complete and they have come from different tombs, but one can put together a kind of composite of what the directions consisted of. (The material is to be found in Jane Harrison's *Prolegomena to the Study of Greek Religion.*)[3]

Thou shalt find on the left of the House of Hades a Well-spring,
And by the side thereof standing a white cypress.
To this Well-spring approach not near.
But thou shalt find another by the Lake of Memory,
Cold water flowing forth, and there are guardians before it.
Say: "I am a child of Earth and of Starry Heaven;
But my race is of Heaven (alone). This ye know yourselves.

And lo, I am parched with thirst and I perish. Give me quickly
The cold water flowing forth from the Lake of Memory."
And of themselves they will give thee to drink from the holy Well-
spring,
And thereafter among the other Heroes thou shalt have lord-
ship. . . .

Another section reads a little differently:

Out of the pure I come, Pure Queen of Them Below,
Eukles and Eubouleus and the other Gods immortal.
For I also avow me that I am of your blessed race,
But Fate laid me low and the other Gods immortal.

Then there is a gap—something about "the starflung thunderbolt"—
and the departed must then say:

I have paid the penalty for deeds unrighteous. . . .
I have flown out of the sorrowful weary Wheel.
I have passed with eager feet to the Circle desired.
I have entered into the bosom of Despoina, Queen of the
Underworld. . . .
Hail, thou who has suffered the Suffering. This thou hadst never
suffered before. . . .
Happy and Blessed One, thou shalt be God instead of mortal.

And the final phrase: "A kid I have fallen into milk." In the first
section we have essentially a single image, the image of a well of
rejuvenating water. It is the same image that is found in the Egyptian
Book of the Dead, in which the departed one is instructed on how to
proceed:

May be opened [to me] the mighty flood by Osiris, and may the abyss
of water be opened [to me]. . . . I have gone round about among the
islands of *Sekhet-Aaru* [a portion of the Elysian fields]. Indefinite time,

without beginning and without end, hath been given to me; I inherit eternity, and everlastingness hath been bestowed upon me.[4]

The message is, I drink the water in the Underworld and I inherit eternity as a result. The image also appears in alchemical symbolism as the water of life, the *aqua vitae* or *aqua permanens*. It is an image of the Self as the center of the psyche that conveys meanings beyond time and space, and so is eternal in a certain sense.

The image comes up again in Jesus' encounter with the Samaritan woman in the gospel of John, in which Jesus says:

> If only you knew what God gives, and who it is that is asking you for a drink, you would have asked him and he would have given you living water . . . whoever drinks the water that I shall give him will never suffer thirst any more. The water that I shall give him will be an inner spring always welling up for eternal life.[5]

That is precisely the archetypal image that is referred to in the Orphic tablet: the departed is instructed to ask for a drink from the well and thereafter will be able to join the fellowship of the immortals. But the Orphic text is more complicated because it speaks of two wells: stay away from the well on the left and go to the well on the right—as though that original image of the well of living water, an image of the Self, had been split into opposites. The two wells can be identified: the left-hand well as Lethe, the waters of forgetfulness, and the right-hand well as Mnemosyne, the waters that promote memory. These images were quite important in ancient times and show up in various texts referring to psychic entities that can still be determined. The water of Lethe actually has an ambiguous role in ancient imagery, sometimes carrying positive connotations and sometimes negative. While in our Orphic text it is clearly something negative, something to be avoided, in other circumstances it is praised. For instance, in Euripides' play, when Orestes is being plagued by the Furies, he says:

> Oh magic of sweet sleep, healer of pain,
> I need thee and how sweetly art thou come.

Oh holy Lethe, wise physician thou
Goddess invoked of miserable men.[6]

The sweet water of forgetfulness is a balm, a soothing thing to someone in misery. The same idea appears in *Macbeth:*

Macbeth does murder sleep—the innocent sleep,
Sleep that knits up the ravell'd sleave of care,
The death of each day's life, sore labour's bath,
Balm of hurt minds, great nature's second course,
Chief nourisher in life's feast.[7]

Such an attitude is not Orphic at all. Jane Harrison says about this
subject:

Orpheus found for "miserable men" another way, not by the vine god
[the vine god leads to forgetfulness] but through the wineless ecstacy
of Mnemosyne [memory]. The Orphic hymn to the goddess ends with
the prayer "And in thy mystics waken memory of the holy rite, and
Lethe drive afar." Lethe is to the Orphic, as to Hesiod, wholly bad, the
thing from which he must purge himself. Plato is thoroughly Orphic
when he says, in the *Phaedrus,* that the soul sinks to earth "full of
forgetfulness and vice." The extreme penalty of the wicked in Erebos
[Hades] is not torture, but unconsciousness *(agnoia)*. Pindar's "slug-
gish streams of murky night," he says, receive the guilty and hide them
in unconsciousness and forgetfulness. . . . "The one and only instrument of punishment is unconsciousness and obscurity, utter disappear-
ance, carrying a man into the smileless river that flows from Lethe,
sinking him into an abyss and yawning gulf, bringing in its train all
obscurity and all unconsciousness."[8]

Against sleep, against wine, Orphic asceticism in a certain sense turns
Dionysian symbolism upside down. The emphasis was on Mnemosyne, and from the psychological standpoint, these ideas make the
Orphics quite modern. Consciousness was the source of salvation,
and consciousness was to be obtained by drinking the waters of recollection, which would evoke memory of the heavenly entities one

had known before one's birth, before drinking the waters of forgetfulness when emerging into material existence. In other words, the
waters of memory open up the archetypal images of the collective
unconscious.

Plato's theory of recollection is similar: to drink the water of memory is to remind us of our heavenly origin. It describes the opposite
process in the "Vision of Er" in *The Republic*—how spirits are prepared for being born onto earth. On their way into birth they must
drink the waters of Lethe; they must become forgetful of their heavenly origin in order to enter the earthly realm. Plato paints this
picture:

> . . . all the souls had chosen their lives in the order of their lots, they
> were marshaled and went before Lachesis. And she sent with each, as
> the guardian of his life and the fulfiller of his choice, the genius that he
> had chosen, and this divinity led the soul first to Clotho, under her
> hand and her turning of the spindle, to ratify the destiny of his lot and
> choice, and after contact with her the genius again led the soul to the
> spinning of Atropos to make the web of its destiny irreversible, and
> then without a backward look it passed beneath the throne of Neces-
> sity. And after it had passed through that . . . they all journeyed to the
> Plain of Oblivion, through a terrible and stifling heat . . . and there
> they camped at eventide by the River of Forgetfulness [that is Lethe]
> whose waters no vessel can contain. They were all required to drink a
> measure of the water, and those who were not saved by their good
> sense drank more than the measure, and each one as he drank forgot
> all things. [All heavenly things. These are spirits coming down from
> heaven on the way to be born into bodies.] And after they had fallen
> asleep and it was the middle of the night, there was a sound of thunder
> and a quaking of the earth, and they were suddenly wafted thence, one
> this way, one that, upward to their birth like shooting stars.[9]

These two waters are like the two gateways referred to in the Cave
of the Nymphs where Odysseus was returned to Ithaca. The cave, it
will be recalled, had two entrances, one for the spirits arriving and
the other for the spirits leaving the earth and returning to heaven.
Those two entrances correspond to the two waters of Lethe and

Mnemosyne; when you enter earthly existence you must forget your archetypal origin, and when you leave your material existence you must drink the water of recollection to return to consciousness of your archetypal origin.

Since this is all projected into the afterlife, it is not recognized as psychological phenomenology; we can best understand these images as referring to the realization of the Self and of the archetypal dimension of the psyche. The infant starts out very largely immersed in the archetypal world, and as he develops an ego he drinks the waters of Lethe, he forgets from whence he came. If he keeps looking back he will never make any place for himself on this actual earth; he has to forget. However, in the later phases of development one must drink the waters of memory in order to recover one's relation to the archetypal and transpersonal origins; only that way can the larger life meanings be found.

"Drinking the waters of Mnemosyne" means to remember the knowledge we once knew, and it is beautifully expressed in the words of the Valentinian Gnostics, giving us a glimpse of how Orphism influenced the later Gnosticism, since all of these ancient cults penetrated one another. Gnostic means "knower" and one might ask the question, what is it the Gnostic knows? This was their answer: "What liberates is the knowledge of who we were, what we became; where we were, whereinto we have been thrown; whereto we speed, wherefrom we are redeemed; what birth is, and what rebirth."[10] What the Gnostic knows according to that formula can be thought of as the essence of what one learns when one drinks the waters of Mnemosyne. The knowledge is the preconscious knowledge of who one was before one came into ego existence, and the same information conveys what one will be after one passes out of ego existence.

The next direction given by the Orphic text is that the initiate must announce: "I am a child of Earth and of Starry Heaven." That is to say he already has to know whence he came. It is like the alchemical notion that to make the philosophers' stone one needs a little bit of it to start with, which is to say that the process is not strictly rational. The Orphic is expected to have acquired the knowledge of whence he came and his announcement will be his entree. "I am a child of

Earth and of Starry Heaven" means psychologically that he is aware of his transpersonal origin; he realizes that his essence does not derive from his personal experience or from what we call his ego being, he has experienced his archetypal individuality. He knows the same sort of thing that Jesus referred to when he said: "Rejoice that your names are written in heaven."[11] This knowledge will permit him to drink the waters of recollection.

Next, he is supposed to announce to the powers he encounters: "Out of the pure I come, Pure Queen of them below" (an allusion to Persephone), and declare "I am pure and I come from out of the pure." The state of being pure held a central place in the ethos of the Orphic communities and was acted out in quite literal forms.

A kindred attitude appears in the Egyptian *Book of the Dead,* where the so-called negative confession goes on for page after page, with the departed one asserting that he has not been guilty of iniquity, has not robbed with violence, nor slain man or woman, nor uttered falsehood, and so on and on. In short, he had to announce that he was pure. Now since we take all this as a projection of an individuation requirement, we must perceive the question of purity, psychologically, as referring to separation from the shadow, the dark and unacceptable content of the personality. Integration of the shadow is a relatively late phenomenon. Much earlier, the ego has to separate itself from the shadow in order to experience itself as good and worthy and distinct from the bad and unworthy and guilty. This is what is happening in the negative confession, where the ego is establishing its worth. Later, it must recognize the opposite, that those earlier statements were only half truths, that it is those negative things in part. Psychological "purity" at this later stage means that one is not contaminated with unconscious factors, not that one does not have a shadow. It means rather, in psychological terms, that one is purified by awareness of the shadow, so that even negative things can be pure if they are accompanied by awareness.

There is of course the implication in such a declaration of purity that a judgment is to be met in the afterlife. The powerful image of the judgment of the soul after death is present in practically all the religions, and is central to Orphism and to the Egyptian religion where there is the image of the soul being weighed in the balance against a feather. The idea of a heavenly accounting points to a profound and irrevocable inner law, which the ego must confront and be judged by, and it corresponds psychologically to the experience of inner judgment, which comes with any significant encounter with the Self, such as Oedipus experienced when the full rush of reality overwhelmed him. Such a judgment can only be made in the presence of an authority other than oneself; the ego cannot judge itself. The expectation of judgment leads to the question of whether or not one will be justified, a whole theological problem. One must keep in mind that these issues did not begin with Christian theology but existed long before the Christian writers picked them up.

In simplest form, the inner archetypal law manifests itself outwardly in the many established codes of behavior, the code of Hammurabi or the Mosaic code or the code of Christian ethics. But such externalizations are not to be mistaken for their inner source, for they are no more than approximations. To the extent that this is recognized, psychological problems become magnified. To the extent that such codes can be taken as a formula to determine how one lives, they simplify the process of living. The Orphics had a code, too, and if their followers obeyed the code, they were considered to be pure, and then the Orphic could announce to the Queen of the Underworld, "Out of the pure I come." Then, the text reads: ". . . Eukles and Eubouleus and the other Gods immortal. / For I also avow me that I am of your blessed race, / But Fate laid me low and the other Gods immortal. / . . . the starflung thunderbolt. . . ." Eukles and Eubouleus are two names for Zagreus—Dionysus as the dismembered one. "I am of your blessed race" refers to the myth of the dismemberment of the infant Dionysus by the Titans. It will be recalled that the Titans ate Dionysus except for his heart, and Zeus then destroyed them with a thunderbolt, but of the ashes man was made, and man thus contains a remnant of the divine spark of Dionysus. The soul declares that he has the Dionysian spark in him because he is made of Titan dust. He should be accepted as a brother of Dionysus, which is simply another way of saying, "I am a child of Starry Heaven"—I have the heavenly light in me. Psychologically that could be paraphrased to mean "I should be admitted to the sacred halls because I am a carrier of transpersonal consciousness."

There follows the gap in the text and the soul next must announce: "I have paid the penalty for deeds unrighteous." Here can be seen the effect of the composite text. This is a more developed statement than the assertion that "I am pure"; the soul does not claim here that it is pure, but rather that it has paid for its unrighteousness, which signifies psychologically that it has accepted the shadow, a much more conscious statement than the negative confession. "I have flown out of the sorrowful weary Wheel."

Pictures of wheels appear in numerous Greek vase paintings of Hades, but there has been little agreement as to what they mean, although some scholars believe they refer to the wheel of Ixion.* It is possible, however, to see these wheels as similar in meaning to the Buddhist wheel of life, the one turned by the pig, the cock, and the serpent, the forces of concupiscence. "The sorrowful weary Wheel" would be the wheel of unconscious wholeness: while the wheel does symbolize totality, as long as it manifests itself on an unconscious basis it is a torture wheel like Ixion's. To fly out of that sorrowful weary wheel might correspond to leaving the state of identification with unconscious wholeness and instead, as is indicated by the next phrase, "I have passed with eager feet to the Circle desired," moving out of one wheel and into relation with another, which could refer to a changed relation to the Self. An unconscious relation to the Self is a sorrowful weary wheel and the circle desired would be a more conscious one. Expressed psychologically, the development of consciousness is a process of first coming out of the crude totality, and then of returning to that circle of totality, consciously.

Actually, the Greek word used here, translated as "circle," is the word that literally means "crown." Hence, we could also have the translation, "I have passed with eager feet to the crown desired," which leads to other associations. "Crowning" was a part of certain mystery initiations, sometimes a brief identification with Helios, the

---

*Ixion was bound by Zeus to a fiery wheel that rolled forever through the sky, as punishment for trying to seduce Hera.

sun god. It refers to the proclaiming of wholeness by the composing of the circle, an image expressed in Paul when he says, as he is contemplating his own upcoming death:

> I have fought the good fight, I have finished the race, I have kept the faith. Henceforth there is laid up for me the crown of righteousness, which the Lord, the righteous judge, will award to me on that Day, and not to me only but also to all who have loved his appearing.[12]

That, in fact, is pure Orphism; the imagery is the same.

We next read: "I have entered into the bosom of Despoina, Queen of the Underworld." *Despoina,* meaning "the mistress," refers here to Persephone, the mistress of the Underworld, and the image refers to a return to the mother for rebirth, a descent into the unconscious. The soul is saying in effect that it has made its descent into the unconscious and therefore is entitled to what comes next—its reward.

Until this point, the initiate has done all the speaking. Now comes a reply and the reply is, "Hail thou who hast suffered the Suffering." The word employed is *pathos,* the same term we encountered in the ritual sequence of the tragedy. Identified by this statement with the tragic hero, the initiate is told, in effect, you are recognized and admitted because you have lived out your tragedy. The focus on suffering as a central value is a prefiguration of Christian symbolism, which emphasizes the significance of the suffering process, for example, in the statement "take up your cross and follow me."

There is a Gnostic image connected with the theme of suffering as a value known as *Jesus patibilis,* the suffering Jesus who is thought to pervade the whole universe, the Jesus who hangs from every tree.[13] It represents the suffering aspect of life as a cosmic phenomenon that in the process of self-realization must undergo evolutionary suffering, so to speak. It is the suffering that brings consciousness, and in the Orphic tablet some supreme value is attached to it, since for the first time the initiate is hailed, and for that particular feat.

Etymologically, the word *suffer* comes from the Latin for "to carry under." The second syllable is the root of the Latin "to carry," and the first derives from the word for "under." The idea being expressed is to get under and hold up from below, to carry from under. Suffering, then, is a carrying and therefore understood not just in terms of pain but in terms of doing the job, doing work. The Orphic is told that you have carried your load and therefore you are entitled to enter.

Then comes his deification, in effect. The initiate has finished his statement and now he is told: "Happy and Blessed One, thou shalt be god instead of mortal." Translated into psychological terms this means that he will become Self rather than ego: all that is personal and ego-centered will be stripped away, leaving the indestructible, eternal, objective reality, which is not subject to mortality, change, or decay. Jung has left us an example of just such an experience on the occasion of his near encounter with death. The vision he describes in his autobiography applies directly to the statement: "Happy and Blessed One, thou shalt be god instead of mortal." In his vision Jung had left the earth and was high above it, approaching a beautiful temple made out of a single block of stone, with the idea that he was to enter it. He writes:

I had the feeling that everything was being sloughed away; everything I aimed at or wished for or thought, the whole phantasmagoria of earthly existence, fell away or was stripped from me—an extremely painful process. Nevertheless, something remained; it was as if I now carried along with me everything I had ever experienced or done, everything that had happened around me. I might also say: it was with me and I was it. I consisted of all that, so to speak. I consisted of my own history, and I felt with great certainty: this is what I am. "I am this bundle of what has been, and what has been accomplished." This experience gave me a feeling of extreme poverty, but at the same time of great fullness. There was no longer anything I wanted or desired. I existed in an objective form; I was what I had been and lived. At first the sense of annihilation predominated, of having been stripped or pillaged; but suddenly that became of no consequence. Everything seemed to be past; what remained was a *fait accompli*, without any reference back to what had been. There was no longer any regret that something had dropped away or been taken away. On the contrary: I had everything that I was, and that was everything.[14]

Although one might assume that the Orphic tablet would end with this, there is a final line. Now the initiate speaks; no longer in the grandiose framework, he has moved directly into the opposite: "A kid, I have fallen into milk." It is a complete reversal. Instead of an immortal god, which is what he has just been proclaimed to be, he is experiencing himself as a tiny, helpless nursling kid in danger of drowning in excessive maternal nourishment—the ego falling back into the universe out of which it came, an image of final innocence, perhaps similar to ". . . unless you turn and become like children, you will never enter the kingdom of heaven."[15] The tablet ends on a common, ordinary, human note rather than a grandiose one, and somehow that feels better.

A good parallel is the Vision of Er in Plato's *Republic,* which shows so many similarities to the Orphic text as to be considered an Orphic document itself. Plato is Orphic through and through, a sophisticated Orphism, and it can be argued that the image of the afterworld of all subsequent theology and philosophy, at least Neo-platonic philosophy, derived from the Vision of Er, which says in part:

> I will tell you a tale . . . about Er, the son of Armenius, a Pamphylian by birth. He was slain in battle, and ten days afterwards, when the bodies of the dead were taken up already in a state of corruption, his body was found unaffected by decay, and carried away home to be buried. On the twelfth day, as he was lying on the funeral pile, he returned to life and told them what he had seen in the other world. He said that when his soul left the body he went on a journey with a great company, and that they came to a mysterious place at which there were two openings in the earth; they were near together, and over against them there were two other openings in the heaven above. In the inter-mediate space there were judges seated, who commanded the just, after they had given judgment on them and had bound their sentences in front of them, to ascend by the heavenly way on the right hand; and in like manner the unjust were bidden by them to descend by the lower way on the left hand; these also bore the symbols of their deeds, but fastened on their backs.

They came to a region where there were two pathways that connected heaven with the depths of the earth. This is a double image of what may be called an ego-Self axis or a connecting link between different aspects of the psyche. Those who were judged unjust were sent down one opening, and those who were judged worthy were shipped up the other opening, an image of judgment also found in the tablets of the Orphics.

> He [Er] drew near, and they told him that he was to be the messenger who would carry the report of the other world to men, and they bade him hear and see all that was to be heard and seen in that place. Then he beheld and saw on one side the souls departing at either opening of heaven and earth when sentence had been given on them; and at the two other openings other souls, some ascending out of the earth dusty and worn with travel, some descending out of heaven clean and bright. And arriving ever and anon they seemed to have come from a long journey, and they went forth with gladness into the meadow, where they encamped as at a festival; and those who knew one another embraced and conversed, the souls which came from earth curiously inquiring about the things above, and the souls which came from heaven about the things beneath. And they told one another what had happened by the way, those from below weeping and sorrowing at the remembrance of the things which they had endured and seen in their journey beneath the earth (now the journey lasted a thousand years), while those from above were describing heavenly delights and visions of inconceivable beauty. The story . . . would take too long to tell; but the sum was this: . . . for every wrong which they had done to anyone they suffered tenfold. . . . If, for example, there were any who had been the cause of many deaths, or had betrayed or enslaved cities or armies, or been guilty of any other evil behavior, for each and all of their offenses they received punishment ten times over, and the rewards of beneficence and justness and holiness were in the same proportion. . . .

It must be kept in mind that what is being described is not the afterlife, which is unknown. The account can be understood as a picture of a double-layered psyche, the heaven and the earth and the depths of the earth containing the area of punishment, with connecting pathways between them. Furthermore, at periodic intervals the psychic contents, the souls that have been occupying heaven, have to leave heaven and come down for reevaluation, and those that have been occupying Hades come up to be reviewed. Those who have been in heaven have become used to the easy life and when it comes time for them to select another existence, they do so carelessly and generally choose a lot that will eventually send them to Hades, whereas those who have been in Hades are wary; they have been through great difficulties and they take their time in making a choice, and hence generally pick something that sends them in time up to heaven. The net effect is circulation, an exchange of places—a provocative image when thought of as a picture of a psychological dynamism.

At this point, a familiar figure appears on the scene, and we have a postscript to the story of Odysseus. All the souls choose their lots and then Plato says:

> There came also the soul Odysseus having yet to make a choice, and his lot happened to be the last of them all. Now the recollection of former toils had disenchanted him of ambition, and he went about for a considerable time in search of the life of a private man who had no cares; he had some difficulty in finding this, which was lying about and had been neglected by everybody else; and when he saw it, he said that he would have done the same had his lot been first instead of last and that he was delighted to have it.[16]

The chief point that Plato makes, in addition to the elegant imagery that we can understand as expressing the structure of the psyche, is the importance of knowing what one is doing, the advisability of having as much consciousness as we can attain. This is how he concludes the vision and ends *The Republic*:

> Wherefore my counsel is that we hold fast ever to the heavenly way and follow after justice and virtue always, considering that the soul is immortal and able to endure every sort of good and every sort of evil. Thus shall we live, dear to one another and to the gods, both while remaining here and when like conquerors in the games, who go around to gather gifts, we receive our reward. And it shall be well with us both

in this life and in the pilgrimage of a thousand years which we have been describing.[17]

One wonders if Paul may have taken his image of the crown of righteousness from this, as well as his symbolic usage of the games, since Plato makes use of the same imagery, "like conquerors in the games."

12

The Eleusinian Mysteries

AMONG THE most remarkable phenomena of the ancient world were the Eleusinian mysteries, which were based on the myth of Demeter and her daughter Persephone. The story relates that Demeter and Persephone were strolling in a meadow where Persephone, who was picking flowers, plucked a narcissus, which was held to be the gateway to the Underworld. The earth sprang open and Hades emerged and carried her off to his realm. Demeter, disconsolate, wandered the earth seeking her. During her absence nothing grew; no seeds sprouted, no leaves came out, no fruit was borne. Everything was sterile and it became evident that mankind would be destroyed if Persephone did not return, so Zeus ordered it. However, a complication arose. She had eaten seven pomegranate seeds while in Hades' kingdom and that committed her to the Underworld; she had a stake in it or it had a stake in her. Finally a compromise was devised under which she was to spend six months of the year above ground

FIG. 26. Persephone returns from beneath the ground, renewing life on earth. She is greeted by Dionysus, Pan, and dancing satyrs; Eros plays the pipes; plants and flowers spring forth. (Transcription by J. Wheelock after a 4th-century BC Attic krater, now lost.)

and six months in the Underworld as the queen of Hades. Meanwhile, during her wanderings, Demeter had stopped at the little village of Eleusis, twelve miles south of Athens, where she was given hospitality by some kindly people, and in return, she had taught her mysteries to the Eleusinians. Such are the bare bones of the myth.

In its most apparent psychological meaning the myth describes a stage of feminine development, the emergence from psychic maidenhood by way of an initial encounter with the masculine. Wrested from her innocent state of daughter and partner of Demeter and plunged into the darkness under the earth, Persephone was suddenly faced with the breakup of the comfortable all-feminine matriarchal condition (as Neumann uses that term).[1] It was torn apart by the appearance of the new masculine principle, represented by Hades. This particular image comes up not uncommonly in young women's dreams. The dreamer of one such dream was in her early twenties:

I'm in a sunny field on the crest of a hill picking flowers for the garland or wreath that will crown my head, for today is my wedding day. There is a female friend with me whom I can't identify. The flowers are exquisitely beautiful, of varieties I've never seen before. I'm very happy. The wedding guests who had gathered here with me have dispersed for the day and will return later for the ceremony. The groom had also gone. I don't know who he was. My mother had fixed my hair by putting it up with flowers but it was all wrong and I became upset and took it down and placed the garland of flowers atop my head. I felt angry that the wedding guests had stayed away for so long as it was already growing late. We gathered in the place where the marriage would take place. This place was aglow with a strange unearthly light, surrounded by a brooding luminous darkness, like the painting of Christ on the cross at his death, when the whole earth quakes and trembles at the meaning of the event.

It should be noted that the unconscious does not duplicate the ancient myth but gives it a Christian twist, with Christian imagery, yet including the original elements of the darkness and the earthquake that is in the offing as the marriage is about to be performed. This image, even to the equation of marriage and death, appears frequently, for example in the story of Amor and Psyche. When the ego of the young woman opens itself to receive the masculine principle for the first time, the whole unconscious seems to open up and this is experienced as a kind of death of the ego, since it involves the loss of the old way as part of the transformation. Dreams of this sort illustrate why purely sexual or even interpersonal interpretations of events such as puberty are inadequate to the psychic realities. One is dealing with another level entirely that is revealed only by such archetypal images as the emergence of Hades from the depths of the earth and, in the case of this modern dream, as the darkness and earthquakes accompanying the crucifixion of Christ.

Here we are looking at the myth of Demeter and Persephone rather specifically and as relevant chiefly to woman's psychology. On a more general level, it is to be read as a death and rebirth mystery, and thus applicable to both men and women, and it was in this wider aspect that it became the foundation for the Eleusinian mysteries, which existed for twelve hundred years. Sworn to strictest secrecy—and the secret was kept—multitudes of people were initiated at Eleusis, including some of the most prominent people of antiquity, Augustus and Marcus Aurelius among them. The rituals were divided into two different categories called the lesser mysteries and the greater mysteries; the former were performed at Agrae, a suburb of Athens, in February, approximately the time that Persephone starts coming to life in the greening of spring; and the latter were celebrated at Eleusis in September, at the time when Persephone is descending into the Underworld.

Thus we have the curious situation that the emergence, the rebirth, was observed as the lesser ritual and the descent as the greater. We may look at the double aspect of the mysteries as corresponding to the two aspects of the psyche as we understand it, what Jung has labeled the personal unconscious and the collective unconscious; dealing with the first we know to be a lesser task, and dealing with the second, a greater task. The lesser mysteries at Agrae consisted largely in purification and instruction, while the greater mysteries, which required that one first go through the lesser ceremonies, lasted about nine days. Further purifications and sacrifices ended in what was called the *epopteia,* a final visionary experience.

A great deal of scholarly effort has been expended seeking to determine what happened in the rituals, since no participant's description has ever come to light. There is reason to believe that some form of sacred marriage was symbolized; some kind of reenactment of Demeter's wanderings, searching for Persephone, and reunion with her was performed, and some form of imagery was presented concerning the birth of the divine child, perhaps symbolized by an ear of wheat. It is known that at the beginning of the greater ceremonies at Eleusis, a solemn warning was issued that those seeking initiation must speak Greek and have pure hands and pure hearts, the same requirement of purity as in Orphism, and indeed it is probable that the Eleusinian mysteries were considerably influenced by Orphic factors. The effects of the initiation seem to have been a psychological regeneration and an experience of renewed life, a sense of meaning and hope. This is most succinctly expressed by suggesting, as Kerényi puts it, that the ultimate purpose of the mysteries was to convey the beatific vision.[2] This connects the Mysteries, like Orphic ritual, with Greek philosophy, which also was considered to have as its ultimate goal the beatific vision.

In the *Phaedrus,* speaking of man's memories of his previous (prenatal) existence, Plato says, "He who employs aright these memories is ever being initiated into perfect mysteries and alone becomes truly perfect." The Greek word for "perfect" *(teleios)* also means "initiate," so another translation could be "becomes a true initiate, the truly complete one."

> But, as he forgets earthly interests and is rapt in the divine, the vulgar deem him mad, and rebuke him; they do not see that he is inspired. . . . For, as has already been said, every soul of man has in the way of nature beheld true being and this was the condition of her passing into the form of man. But all souls do not easily recall the things of the other world; they may have seen them for a short time only, or they may have been unfortunate in their earthly lot, and having had their hearts turned to unrighteousness through some corrupting influence, they may have lost the memory of the holy things which once they saw. Few only retain an adequate remembrance of them; and they, when they behold here any image of that other world, are rapt in amazement; but they are ignorant of what this rapture means, because they do not clearly perceive. For there is no light of justice or temperance or any of the higher ideas which are precious to souls in the earthly copies of them: they are seen through a glass dimly; and there are few who going to the images, behold in them the realities, and these only with difficulty. There was a time when with the rest of the happy band they saw beauty shining in brightness,—we philosophers following in the train of Zeus, others in company with other gods; and then we beheld the beatific vision and were initiated into a mystery which may be truly called most blessed, celebrated by us in our state of innocence, before we had any experience of evils to come, when we were admitted to the sight of apparitions innocent and simple and calm and happy, which we beheld shining in pure light. . . .[3]

Plato thus specifically identifies the philosophers with those initiated into the mysteries. This particular passage has been interpreted as indicating that apparitions were generated and displayed in the Eleusinian mysteries, assuming that Plato knew about the mysteries and is alluding to what happened in them in a veiled way. While that cannot be proved or disproved, the passage nevertheless forms a link between the two cultural forms—the mysteries and the philosophical systems, and is useful as one attempts to trace the basic archetypal images as they manifest themselves in progressively more differentiated forms through the history of Western culture. From the elemental myths, into their religious and ritual expressions such as Orphism, into the philosophical manifestations, and then branching out into such diverse areas as alchemy, Christian theology, and modern depth psychology, the thread can be followed.

The basic effect of the mysteries seemed to be that they reconciled the participants to life and in that sense were redeeming. For instance, in the "Homeric Hymn to Demeter," we find: "Happy is he among men on earth who has seen these mysteries; but he who is uninitiate and who has no part in them, never has lot of like good things once he is dead, down in the darkness and gloom."[4] Although the sense of redemption is projected into the afterworld, that is nonetheless the nature of the actual experience. It seems that the initiation into the mysteries conveyed a new awareness of the nature of life— some kind of insight into the transcendent dimension of being that was primarily reassuring and generated hope. Hope is repeatedly spoken of as one of the effects of the initiation; it was one of the consequences of the beatific vision.

These themes come up in one of a series of dreams of a man who was to die several months later:

I was with several companions in a Daliesque landscape where things seemed either imprisoned or out of control. There were fires all about coming out of the ground and about to engulf the place. By a group effort, we managed to control the fires and restrict them to their proper place. In the same landscape, we found a woman lying on her back on a rock. The front side of her body was flesh, but the back of her head and body was part of the living rock on which she lay. She had a dazzling smile, almost beatific. It seemed to accept her plight. The controlling of the fire seemed to have caused a metamorphosis of some kind and began a loosening of the rock at her back so that we were finally able to lift her off. Although she was still partly stone, she did not seem too heavy and the change was continuing. We knew that she would be whole again.

What makes the dream relevant in this context is that the setting, and the fires in particular, reminded the dreamer of the fire that was said to accompany Hades when he broke out of the earth to capture Persephone. The dreamer had once visited Eleusis and had been shown the spot where Hades was supposed to have emerged. That was his first association to the dream. Kerényi[5] has demonstrated that sacred fire was one of the features of the Eleusinian mysteries and of course the beatific smile of the woman is an allusion to the beatific vision. The dream carried a sense of reassurance with it.

We can best relate to these mysteries, perhaps, by taking a few examples of what can be considered their modern counterparts. We have no collective or ceremonial equivalent to the Eleusinian mysteries today, but we can find in psychotherapy and in literature and biography examples that are analogous to what presumably happened at Eleusis. Here is a dream that can be taken as a modern equivalent of the beatific vision. It is a dream of J. B. Priestley's, quoted in his book *Rain Upon Godshill* and reproduced in Gerhard Adler's *Studies in Analytical Psychology*:

I dreamt I was standing at the top of a very high tower, alone, looking down upon myriads of birds all flying in one direction; every kind of bird was there, all the birds in the world. It was a noble sight, this vast aerial river of birds. But now in some mysterious fashion the gear was changed, and time speeded up, so that I saw generations of birds, watched them break their shells, flutter into life, mate, weaken, falter, and die. Wings grew only to crumble; bodies were sleek and then, in a flash, bled and shrivelled; and death struck everywhere at every second. What was the use of all this blind struggle towards life, this eager trying of wings, this hurried mating, this flight and surge, all this gigantic meaningless biological effort? As I stared down, seeming to see every creature's ignoble little history almost at a glance, I felt sick at heart.

It would be better if not one of them, if not one of us all, had been born, if the struggle ceased for ever. I stood on my tower, still alone, desperately unhappy. But now the gear was changed again, and time went faster still, and it was rushing by at such a rate, that the birds could not show any movement, but were like an enormous plain sown with feathers. But along this plain, flickering through the bodies themselves, there now passed a sort of white flame, trembling, dancing, then hurrying on; and as soon as I saw it I knew that this white flame was life itself, the very quintessence of being; and then it came to me, in a rocket-burst of ecstasy, that nothing mattered, nothing could ever matter, because nothing else was real, but this quivering and hurrying lambency of being. Birds, men, or creatures not yet shaped and colored, all were of no account except so far as this flame of life travelled through them. It left nothing to mourn over behind it; what I had thought was tragedy was mere emptiness or a shadow show; for now all real feeling was caught and purified and danced on ecstatically with the white flame of life.[6]

Another example comes from Jung's visions and their aftermath, which appear to be about the same level of experience as the ancient material itself. During Jung's long weeks of convalescence after the *basileus* of Kos in the form of his physician had brought him back to life, he had experiences that are modern analogies of the beatific vision of the Eleusinian mysteries:

During those weeks I lived in a strange rhythm. By day I was usually depressed. I felt weak and wretched, and scarcely dared to stir. Gloomily, I thought, "Now I must go back to this drab world." Toward evening I would fall asleep, and my sleep would last until about midnight. Then I would come to myself and lie awake for about an hour, but in an utterly transformed state. It was as if I were in ecstasy. I felt as though I were floating in space, as though I were safe in the womb of the universe—in a tremendous void, but filled with the highest possible feeling of happiness. "This is eternal bliss," I thought. "This cannot be described; it is far too wonderful!" . . . [I seemed to be] in the Pardes Rimmonim, the garden of pomegranates [a note in the text tells us that this is the title of an old Cabbalistic tract; it is the place where Malchuth and Tifereth, two aspects of the deity, appear], and the wedding of Tifereth with Malchuth was taking place. Or else I was Rabbi Simon ben Jochai, whose wedding in the afterlife was being celebrated. It was the mystic marriage as it appears in the Cabbalistic tradition. I cannot tell you how wonderful it was. I could only think continually, "Now this is the garden of pomegranates! Now this is the marriage of Malchuth with Tifereth!" . . . And my beatitude was that of a blissful wedding.

Gradually the garden of pomegranates faded away and changed. There followed the Marriage of the Lamb, in a Jerusalem festively bedecked. I cannot describe what it was like in detail. These were ineffable states of joy. Angels were present, and light. I myself was the "Marriage of the Lamb."

That, too, vanished, and there came a new image, the last vision. I walked up a wide valley to the end, where a gentle chain of hills began. The valley ended in a classical amphitheater. It was magnificently situated in the green landscape. And there, in this theater, the *hierosgamos* [the sacred wedding] was being celebrated. Men and women dancers came on stage, and upon a flower-decked couch All-father Zeus and Hera consummated the mystic marriage, as it is described in the *Iliad*.

All these experiences were glorious. Night after night I floated in a state of purest bliss, "thronged round with images of all creation. . . ." It is impossible to convey the beauty and intensity of emotion during those visions. They were the most tremendous things I have ever experienced.[7]

Finally, there is Dante's vision, with which he concludes *The Divine Comedy,* and which is parallel to Jung's and to what may have been the beatific vision experienced by at least a few in the Eleusinian mysteries:

O Light Supreme, that art so far exalted
Above our mortal ken! Lend to my mind
A little part of what Thou didst appear,

And grant sufficient power unto my tongue
That it may leave for races yet unborn,
A single spark of Thy almighty flame!

For if Thou wilt come back to my remembrance,
That I may sing Thy glory in these lines,
The more Thy victory will be explained.

I think the keenness of the living ray
That I withstood would have bewildered me,
If once my eyes had turned aside from it.

And I recall that for that very reason
I was emboldened to endure so much,
Until my gaze was joined unto His good.

Abundant grace, by which I could presume
To fix my eyes upon the Eternal Light,
Sufficiently to see the whole of it!

I saw that in its depths there are enclosed
Bound up with love in one eternal book,
The scattered leaves of all the universe—

Substance, and accidents, and their relations,
As though together fused in such a way
That what I speak of is a single light.

The universal form of this commingling,
I think I saw, for when I tell of it,
I feel that I rejoice so much the more. . . .

For within the substance, deep and radiant,
Of that Exalted Light, I saw three rings
Of one dimension, yet of triple hue.

One seemed to be reflected by the next,
As Iris is by Iris; and the third
Seemed fire, shed forth equally by both.

How powerless is speech—how weak compared
To my conception, which itself is trifling
Beside the mighty vision that I saw!

Oh Light Eternal, in Thyself contained!
Thou only know'st Thyself and in Thyself
Both known and knowing, smilest on Thyself!

That very circle which appeared in Thee,
Conceived as but reflection of a light,
When I had gazed on it awhile, now seemed

To bear the image of the human face
Within itself, of its own coloring—
Wherefore my sight was wholly fixed on it.

Like a geometer, who will attempt
With all his power and mind to square the circle,
Yet cannot find the principle he needs:

Just so was I, at that phenomenon.
I wished to see how image joined to ring,
And how the one found place within the other.

Too feeble for such flights were my own wings;
But by a lightning flash my mind was struck—
And thus came the fulfillment of my wish.

My power now failed that phantasy sublime:
My will and my desire were both revolved,
As is a wheel in even motion driven

By Love, which moves the sun and other stars.[8]

Notes

The abbreviation CW in the notes refers to *The Collected Works of C. G. Jung.* The abbreviation MDR refers to Jung's *Memories, Dreams, Reflections.* Quotes from the Bible are noted as NEB (New English Bible), AV (Authorized [King James] Version), or RSV (Revised Standard Version).

EDITOR'S PREFACE

1. *Aion,* lecture series available on tape from the C. G. Jung Institute, Los Angeles.

2. *Parabola,* vol. 1, no. 1, 1976.

Chapter 1. WHAT IS MYTHOLOGY?

1. C. G. Jung, *Symbols of Transformation,* vol. 5 of *The Collected Works* [CW] *of C. G. Jung* (Princeton, N.J.: Princeton Univ. Press, 1950, 1984), par. 466.

2. E.g., *The Greek Myths* (Baltimore: Penguin, 1955).

3. Homer, *The Iliad of Homer,* trans. Alexander Pope (New York: Macmillan, 1965), VI, line 6.

4. John Milton, "Lycidas," lines 70–84.

5. John Keats, "Endymion," lines 1–24.

6. Ovid, *Metamorphoses,* trans. Rolfe Humphries (Bloomington: Indiana Univ. Press, 1955), p. 204.

Chapter 2. THE BEGINNINGS: COSMOGONY

1. Henry Wadsworth Longfellow, "Prometheus," lines 11–25, 56–65.

2. Aeschylus, *Prometheus Bound,* trans. E. D. A. Morshead, in *The Complete Greek Drama I,* ed. W. J. Oates and Eugene O'Neill (New York: Random House, 1950), lines 437–504.

3. Isa. 53:2–6 (NEB).

Chapter 3. THE OLYMPIAN GODS

1. Homer, *The Odyssey,* trans. A. T. Murray (Cambridge, Mass.: Harvard Univ. Press/Loeb Classical Library, 1984), VI, 41–46.

2. Richard Wilhelm, trans., *The I Ching or Book of Changes,* trans. from the German by Cary F. Baynes (New York: Pantheon, 1950), p. 1.

3. Plato, *The Republic,* in *The Dialogues of Plato,* trans. Benjamin Jowett (New York: Random House, 1937), Book 3.

4. Wilhelm, *The I Ching,* p. 210.

5. Percy Bysshe Shelley, "Hymn of Apollo," lines 13–18, 31–36.

6. Heraclitus, fragment 53, in Kathleen Freeman, *Ancilla to the Pre-Socratic Philosophers* (Cambridge, Mass.: Harvard Univ. Press, 1962), p. 28.

7. Hesiod, "Hymn to Ares," in *The Homeric Hymns,* trans. Charles Boer (Irving, Tex.: Spring Publications, 1979), lines 1–43.

Chapter 4. THE OLYMPIAN GODDESSES

1. Lucretius, *Of the Nature of Things,* trans. W. E. Leonard (New York: E. P. Dutton and Sons/Everyman Library, 1943), I, lines 1–25.

2. Euripides, *Hippolytus,* in *The Complete Greek Drama I,* lines 442–450.

3. Prov. 8:22–31 (NEB).

Chapter 5. THE HEROES

1. Jung, *Psychological Types,* CW 6 (1971), par. 757.

2. Ibid., par. 755.

3. Otto Rank, *The Myth of the Birth of the Hero* (New York: Vintage Books, 1959), p. 65.

4. Louis Ginsberg, *Legends of the Bible* (Philadelphia: Jewish Publication Society of America, 1975), pp. 288f.

5. Friedrich Nietzsche, "Homer's Contest," in *The Portable Nietzsche,* ed. Walter Kaufman (New York: Viking Press, 1974), p. 33.

6. Sophocles, *Oedipus at Colonus,* trans. R. C. Jebbs, in *The Complete Greek Drama I,* lines 1224–1228.

7. Erich Neumann, *The Origins and History of Consciousness* (New York: Bollingen Foundation, 1954), p. 42.

8. Sophocles, *Antigone,* trans. R. C. Jebbs, in *The Complete Greek Drama I,* lines 943–949.

9. William Shakespeare, *Hamlet,* 3.2.20–24.

10. Arthur Schopenhauer, *The World as Will and Representation,* vol. 1, trans. E. F. J. Payne (Indian Hills, Colo.: Falcon's Wing Press, 1958), p. 85.

Chapter 6. THE TROJAN WAR

1. Jung, *Psychology and Alchemy,* CW 12 (1953, 1968), p. 51.

2. Gilbert Murray, *The Rise of the Greek Epic* (London: Oxford Univ. Press, 1907), p. 224.

3. Christopher Marlowe, *The Tragedy of Doctor Faustus,* ed. Louis B. Wright (New York: Washington Square Press, 1959), Sc. 13, l. 106–126.

4. Johann Wolfgang von Goethe, *Faust,* trans. Louis MacNeice (New York: Galaxy Book/Oxford Univ. Press, 1960), p. 303.

5. Aeschylus, *Agamemnon,* trans. E. D. A. Morshead, in *The Complete Greek Drama,* lines 916–925.

6. Murray, *The Rise of the Greek Epic,* p. 264f.

7. Homer, *The Iliad,* I, lines 1–8.

8. Sigmund Freud, quoted in Ernest Jones, *The Life and Work of Sigmund Freud,* vol. 1 (New York: Basic Books, 1953), p. 5.

9. Homer, *The Iliad,* I, lines 378–383.

10. Ibid., XXIV, lines 622–662.

Chapter 7. ODYSSEUS

1. Homer, *The Odyssey,* IX, lines 39–60.

2. Jung, *The Structure and Dynamics of the Psyche,* CW 8 (1960, 1969), par. 778.

3. Homer, *The Odyssey*, IX, lines 94–99.

4. Alfred Tennyson, "The Lotos-Eaters," lines 37–45.

5. Jung, *The Practice of Psychotherapy*, CW 16 (1974), par. 489.

6. Homer, *The Odyssey*, IX, lines 106–115.

7. Hesiod, *Works and Days*, trans. Hugh Evelyn-White, in *The Homeric Hymns and Homerica* (Cambridge, Mass.: Harvard Univ. Press/Loeb Classical Library, 1959), lines 112–122.

8. Erich Neumann, *Origins and History of Consciousness*, pp. 266–275.

9. Homer, *The Odyssey*, X, lines 289–298.

10. Ibid., X, lines 302–306.

11. Cleanthes, fragment 526, quoted in Hugo Rahner, *Greek Myths and Christian Mystery* (New York: Biblo and Tannen, 1971), p. 193.

12. Heraclitus, *Homeric Problems*, 73, quoted in Rahner, *Greek Myths and Christian Mystery*, p. 194.

13. Homer, *The Odyssey*, X, lines 496–498.

14. Dante Alighieri, *The Divine Comedy*, trans. Lawrence Grant White (New York: Pantheon, 1948), *Inferno* I, lines 1–7.

15. Goethe, *Faust*, p. 20f.

16. Herman Melville, *Moby-Dick* (New York: Modern Library, 1926), p. 1.

17. Nietzsche, "Mixed Opinions and Maxims," in *The Basic Writings of Nietzsche*, trans. and ed. Walter Kaufman (New York: Modern Library/Random House, 1968), p. 159.

18. Virgil, *The Aeneid of Virgil*, trans. Rolfe Humphries (New York: Charles Scribner's Sons, 1953), VI, lines 243–249.

19. Ibid., VI, lines 260–294.

20. Ibid., VI, lines 724–751.

21. Homer, *The Odyssey*, XII, lines 184–191.

22. Plato, *The Republic*, X, 617.

23. Jung, *Memories, Dreams, Reflections* [MDR], ed. Aniela Jaffé (New York: Random House, 1963), p. 189.

24. Plato, *The Republic*, X, 619B.

25. Plato, *Laws*, in *Collected Dialogues of Plato*, ed. Edith Hamilton and Huntington Cairns (New York: Pantheon, 1961), VII, 792D.

26. *Wo aber Gefahr ist, Wächst Das Rettende auch.* Translated by the author from Friedrich Hölderlin, "Patmos," in *Poems and Fragments* (Ann Arbor: Univ. of Michigan Press, 1967), p. 462.

27. Homer, *The Odyssey,* VIII, lines 550–563.

28. Ibid., XIII, lines 96–112.

29. Porphyry, *On the Cave of the Nymphs,* trans. Robert Lamberton (Barrytown, N.Y.: Station Hill, 1983), parts 20 and 23.

Chapter 8. THE TRAGIC DRAMA: OEDIPUS

1. Aristotle, *Poetics,* trans. W. Hamilton Fyfe (Cambridge, Mass.: Harvard Univ. Press; London: William Heinemann, 1965), 6.3.

2. Jung, *Mysterium Coniunctionis,* CW 14 (1965, 1970), par. 778.

3. Gilbert Murray, "Excursus in the Ritual Forms Preserved in Greek Tragedy," in Jane Harrison, *Themis* (London: Cambridge Univ. Press, 1927), pp. 341ff.

4. A. C. Bradley, *Shakespearean Tragedy* (Greenwich, Conn.: Fawcett Publications/Premier Books, 1965), p. 27.

5. Ibid., p. 29.

6. Jung, *Symbols of Transformation,* CW 5, pars. 264f.

7. Sophocles, *Oedipus the King,* in *The Oedipus Plays of Sophocles,* trans. Paul Roche (New York: Penguin, 1991), lines 20–26.

8. Ibid., lines 37–51.

9. Ibid., lines 1188–1191.

10. Ibid., lines 411–419.

11. John Bunyan, *Grace Abounding to the Chief of Sinners* (Oxford: Clarendon Press, 1962), p. 27.

12. Martin Luther, quoted in Roland Bainton, *Here I Stand* (New York: Abingdon-Cokesbury, 1950), pp. 82f.

13. Sophocles, *Oedipus at Colonus,* lines 1516–1544.

14. Sophocles, *Antigone,* lines 1346–1350.

Chapter 9. SHRINES AND ORACLES

1. C. A. Meier, *Ancient Incubation and Modern Psychotherapy* (Evanston, Ill.: Northwestern Univ. Press, 1967), pp. 53–61.

2. Jung, MDR, pp. 292f.

3. Plutarch, "De genio Socratis," *Moralia* VII, trans. P. H. De Lacy and B. Einarson (Cambridge, Mass.: Harvard Univ. Press/Loeb Classical Library, 1968), 591B.

4. Jung, *Mysterium Coniunctionis,* CW 14, par. 173.

5. Plutarch, "De genio Socratis," 591.

Chapter 10. DIONYSUS

1. Heb. 10:31 (AV).

2. Euripides, *The Bacchae,* in *The Bacchae and Other Plays,* trans. Philip Vellacott (New York: Penguin Books, 1973), lines 298–301.

3. Euripides, quoted in Jane Harrison, *Prolegomena to the Study of Greek Religion* (New York: Meridian Books, 1957), p. 479.

4. Clement of Alexandria, quoted in Harrison, *Prolegomena,* p. 483.

5. Proclus, *Timaeus* 3, quoted in G. R. S. Mead, *Orpheus* (London: John Watkins, 1965), pp. 160ff.

6. Percy Bysshe Shelley, "Adonais," lines 450–463.

7. Alan Watts, *Myth and Ritual in Christianity* (Boston: Beacon Press, 1968), p. 155.

8. Jung, *Nietzsche's Zarathustra,* ed. J. L. Jarrett (Princeton, N.J.: Princeton Univ. Press, 1988), pp. 57f.

9. Edward Fitzgerald, trans., *The Rubaiyat of Omar Khayyam* (Mount Vernon: Peter Pauper Press, 1937), verses 40 and 43.

10. John Milton, "Comus," lines 63–77.

11. William Blake, *The Marriage of Heaven and Hell,* The Voice of the Devil.

12. Milton, "Comus," lines 722–755.

13. Jung, *Psychology and Alchemy,* CW 12, par. 179.

14. Nietzsche, *The Birth of Tragedy,* in *Basic Writings of Nietzsche,* p. 37.

15. Eph. 2:13–15 (RSV).

16. 1 Cor. 11:27 (NEB).

17. Euripides, *The Bacchae,* line 18.

Chapter 11. ORPHISM

1. For a definition of *thyrsus,* see the glossary.

2. Plato, *Phaedo,* in *Plato,* trans. H. N. Fowler (Cambridge, Mass.: Harvard Univ. Press/Loeb Classical Library, 1962), 69B–D.

3. Quoted in Harrison, *Prolegomena,* pp. 573–585.

4. E. A. Wallis Budge, *The Book of the Dead,* vol. 2 (London: Routledge and Kegan Paul, 1949), p. 207.

5. John 4:10, 14 (NEB).

6. Euripides, *Orestes,* line 211, quoted in Harrison, *Prolegomena.*

7. Shakespeare, *Macbeth,* 2.2.35–39.

8. Harrison, *Prolegomena,* pp. 581f.

9. Plato, *The Republic,* X, 620E–621B.

10. Quoted in Hans Jonas, *The Gnostic Religion* (Boston: Beacon Press, 1963), p. 45.

11. Luke 10:17 (RSV).

12. 2 Tim. 4:7–8 Standard Edition.

13. Jonas, *The Gnostic Religion,* pp. 228f.

14. Jung, MDR, pp. 290f.

15. Matt. 18:3 (RSV).

16. Plato, *The Republic,* X, 614B–620D.

17. Ibid., 621B.

Chapter 12. THE ELEUSINIAN MYSTERIES

1. Neumann, *The Origins and History of Consciousness,* pp. 41ff.

2. Carl Kerényi, *Eleusis* (Princeton, N.J.: Princeton Univ. Press, 1988), pp. 95–102.

3. Plato, *Phaedrus,* in *The Dialogues of Plato,* 249C–250C.

4. Hesiod, *The Homeric Hymns and Homerica,* lines 480–482.

5. Kerényi, *Eleusis,* pp. 92f.

6. J. B. Priestley, *Rain Upon Godshill,* quoted in Gerhard Adler, *Studies in Analytical Psychology* (London: Routledge and Kegan Paul, 1948), p. 143.

7. Jung, MDR, pp. 293ff.

8. Dante Alighieri, *The Divine Comedy, Paradiso,* 33, lines 67–145.

Glossary

ACTIVE IMAGINATION A technique for conscious dialogue between the ego and the unconscious whereby unconscious contents are integrated. See C. G. Jung, *Mysterium Coniunctionis,* pars. 752ff.

ANIMA Latin, fem., "soul." The unconscious, feminine side of a man's personality. She is personified in dreams by images of women ranging in nature from harlot and seductress to divine Wisdom and spiritual guide. Identification with the anima causes a man to become effeminate, sulky, and resentful. Projection of the anima accounts for a man's falling in love.

ANIMUS Latin, masc., "soul." The unconscious masculine side of a woman's personality. He is the logos spirit principle in women. When identified with the animus, a woman becomes argumentative and rigidly opinionated. Projection of the animus leads to a woman's falling in love.

ARCHETYPE, ARCHETYPAL IMAGE A universal and recurring image, pattern, or motif representing a typical human experience. Archetypal images come from the collective unconscious and are the basic contents of religions, mythologies, legends, and fairy tales. They also emerge from the collective unconscious in individuals through dreams and visions. Encounter with an archetypal image evokes a strong emotional reaction, conveying a sense of divine or transpersonal power that transcends the ego.

ASSOCIATION The spontaneous flow of interconnected thoughts and images following from a specific idea. Associations are determined by unconscious, meaningful connections and are never fortuitous.

COAGULATIO   An alchemical term related to the personal realization of an archetypal image. This implies that a piece of the collective unconscious has become connected with the ego consciousness of an individual person and is expressed in his or her concrete earthly life.

COLLECTIVE UNCONSCIOUS   The deepest layer of the unconscious, which is ordinarily inaccessible to awareness. Its nature is suprapersonal, universal, and nonindividual. Its manifestations are experienced as alien to the ego, numinous, or divine. The contents of the collective unconscious are the archetypes and their specific symbolic representations, archetypal images.

COMPLEX   An emotionally charged unconscious entity composed of a number of associated ideas grouped around a central core that is an archetypal image. One recognizes that a complex has been activated when emotion upsets psychic balance and disturbs the customary function of the ego.

CONIUNCTIO   A term from alchemy referring to the archetypal image of the sacred marriage or union of opposites. It signifies the goal of individuation, the conscious realization of the Self.

EGO   The center of consciousness and the seat of the individual's experience of subjective identity.

EXTRAVERSION   A mode of psychic functioning in which interest, value, and meaning are attached primarily to external objects. Inner subjective matters are given little worth. Opposite of introversion.

FEELING   One of the four psychic functions according to Jung. It is the rational (i.e., judgmental) function that determines value and promotes personal relationship.

FUNCTION, INFERIOR   That psychological function least developed in a particular individual. It expresses itself in primitive, archaic, and affect-laden ways. The inferior function is the gateway to the collective unconscious.

FUNCTION, SUPERIOR   The most highly developed and differentiated of the psychological functions in a particular individual.

FUNCTIONS, PSYCHOLOGICAL   There are four modes of psychic adaptation according to Jung: thinking, feeling, sensation, and intuition (q.v.).

IDENTIFICATION   Believing oneself to be the same as another person or as an archetypal entity. The process occurs unconsciously, thus differing from imitation, and hinders the awareness of one's true individuality. When the identification is with an archetypal image, inflation (q.v.) results.

INDIVIDUATION The conscious realization and fulfillment of one's unique being. It is associated with typical archetypal imagery and leads to the experiencing of the Self as the center of personality transcending the ego. It begins with one or more decisive experiences challenging egocentricity and producing the awareness that the ego is subordinate to a more comprehensive psychic entity.

INFLATION A psychic state characterized by an exaggerated and unreal sense of one's own importance. It is caused by an identification of the ego with an archetypal image.

INTROVERSION A mode of psychic functioning in which interest, value, and meaning are found predominantly in the inner life of the individual. Values are determined largely by the subject's internal reactions. Opposite of extraversion.

INTUITION One of the four psychic functions according to Jung. It is perception via the unconscious, i.e., perception of contents or conclusions whose origin is obscure.

LIBIDO The psychic energy that motivates the psyche. Interest, attention, and drive are all expressions of libido. The libido invested in a given item is indicated by the quantity of its "value-charge," either positive or negative.

MANDALA Sanskrit, "magic circle." In analytical psychology, an archetypal image representing the Self. The basic mandala is a circle with a square or other fourfold structure superimposed. Mandalas are found in the culture-products of all races. They seem to represent a central integrating principle that lies at the root of the psyche.

NEKYIA A term borrowed from Homer's *Odyssey* signifying a descent to the Underworld; in psychological terms, an encounter with the collective unconscious.

NUMINOSUM, NUMINOUS First used by Rudolf Otto to describe the experience of the divine as awesome, terrifying, and "wholly other." In analytical psychology, it is used to describe the ego's experience of an archetype, especially the Self.

OBJECTIVE PSYCHE See collective unconscious.

PRIMA MATERIA An alchemical term meaning "original matter." It is the psychological stuff that one starts with, the inflated immaturities of one's own psyche, which contain the basic material for the realization of individuality.

PROJECTION   The process whereby an unconscious quality or content of one's own is perceived and reacted to in an outer object.

QUATERNITY   The archetype of fourfoldness symbolizing wholeness. It is closely associated with representations of the Self.

SELF   The central and comprehensive archetype expressing the totality of the psyche as organized around a dynamic center. It is commonly symbolized by a mandala or a paradoxical union of opposites. The Self is experienced as the objective, transpersonal center of identity that transcends the ego. Empirically it cannot be distinguished from the image of God.

SENSATION   One of the four psychic functions according to Jung. It is that function that perceives and adapts to external reality via the senses.

SHADOW   An unconscious part of the personality usually containing inferior characteristics and weaknesses that the individual's self-esteem will not permit him to recognize as his own. It is the first layer of the unconscious to be encountered in psychological analysis and is personified in dreams by dark and dubious figures of the same sex as the dreamer.

SHADOW, ARCHETYPAL   Refers to the experience of impersonal general weakness, inferiority, or evil that is common to humankind. It has been expressed in the figure of the devil and in the concept of humans as miserable sinners.

SYNCHRONICITY   A term coined by Jung for a postulated acausal connecting principle to explain the occurrence of meaningful coincidence, i.e., whenever an inner psychic happening (dream, vision, premonition) is accompanied by a corresponding outer physical event that could not have been causally connected with the former. Most cases of extrasensory perception are considered to be examples of synchronicity.

THINKING   One of the four psychic functions according to Jung. It is the rational capacity to structure and synthesize discrete data by means of categories and conceptual generalizations.

THYRSUS   The fennel stalk, wound with ivy, used as a staff in the rites of Dionysus.

UNCONSCIOUS, THE   That portion of the psyche which is outside conscious awareness. The unconscious expresses itself in dreams, phantasies, obsessive preoccupations, slips of the tongue, and accidents of all kinds. Jung distinguishes two layers of the unconscious: the personal unconscious derived from the personal experience of the individual, and the collective unconscious containing the universal patterns and images called archetypes which are shared by all humans.

UROBOROS   The original psychic state of wholeness, seen in earliest infancy, prior to the birth of ego consciousness. It is symbolized by the circular image of the tail-eating serpent.

WHOLENESS   A condition in which the differing—and often opposing—parts of the personality, including consciousness and the unconscious, are brought into a vital unity. Jung emphasizes a distinction between wholeness and perfection.

Bibliography

Adler, Gerhard. *Studies in Analytical Psychology.* London: Routledge and Kegan Paul, 1948.

Aeschylus. *Agamemnon,* trans. E. D. A. Morshead, in *The Complete Greek Drama I,* ed. W. J. Oates and Eugene O'Neill. New York: Random House, 1950.

———. *Prometheus Bound,* trans. Paul Elmer More, in *The Complete Greek Drama I,* ed. W. J. Oates and Eugene O'Neill. New York: Random House, 1950.

Aristotle, *Poetics,* trans. W. Hamilton Fyfe. Cambridge: Harvard Univ. Press; London: William Heinemann, 1965.

Bainton, Roland. *Here I Stand.* New York: Abingdon-Cokesbury, 1950.

Bradley, A. C. *Shakespearean Tragedy.* Greenwich, Conn.: Fawcett Publications, Premier Books, 1965.

Budge, E. A. Wallis. *The Book of the Dead,* vol. 2. London: Routledge and Kegan Paul, 1949.

Bunyan, John. *Grace Abounding to the Chief of Sinners.* Oxford: Clarendon Press, 1962.

Clement of Alexandria, quoted in Jane Harrison, *Prolegomena to the Study of Greek Religion.* New York: Meridian Books, 1957.

Dante Alighieri. *The Divine Comedy,* trans. Lawrence Grant White. New York: Pantheon, 1948.

Edinger, Edward F. *Ego and Archetype*. New York: G. P. Putnam's Sons, 1972.

Euripides. *The Bacchae*, in *The Bacchae and Other Plays*, trans. Philip Vellacott. New York: Penguin Books, 1973.

———. *The Bacchae*, in *The Complete Greek Tragedies, Euripides*, vol. 4, ed. David Grene and Richmond Lattimore. Chicago: Univ. of Chicago Press, 1960.

———. *Hippolytus*, in *The Complete Greek Drama I*, ed. W. J. Oates and Eugene O'Neill. New York: Random House, 1950.

———. *Orestes*, quoted by Jane Harrison in *Prolegomena to the Study of Greek Religion*. New York: Meridian Books, 1957.

Fitzgerald, Edward, trans., *The Rubaiyat of Omar Khayyam*. Mount Vernon: Peter Pauper Press, 1937.

Freeman, Kathleen. *Ancilla to the Pre-Socratic Philosophers*. Cambridge: Harvard Univ. Press, 1962.

Ginsberg, Louis. *Legends of the Bible*. Philadelphia: Jewish Publication Society of America, 1975.

Goethe, Johann Wolfgang von. *Faust*, trans. Louis MacNeice. New York: Galaxy Book/Oxford Univ. Press, 1960.

Graves, Robert. *The Greek Myths*. Penguin Books, 1955.

Harrison, Jane. *Prolegomena to the Study of Greek Religion*. New York: Meridian Books, 1957.

Heraclitus. *Homeric Problems*, quoted in Hugo Rahner, *Greek Myths and Christian Mystery*. New York: Biblo and Tannen, 1971.

Hesiod. "Homeric Hymn to Demeter," trans. Hugh Evelyn-White, in *The Homeric Hymns and Homerica*. Loeb Classical Library. Cambridge, Mass.: Harvard Univ. Press, 1959.

———. "Hymn to Ares," trans. Charles Boer, in *The Homeric Hymns*. Irving, Tex.: Spring Publications, 1979.

———. *Works and Days*, trans. Hugh Evelyn-White, in *The Homeric Hymns and Homerica*. Loeb Classical Library. Cambridge: Harvard Univ. Press, 1959.

Hölderlin, Friedrich. "Patmos," in *Poems and Fragments*, trans. Michael Hamburger. Ann Arbor, Mich.: Univ. of Michigan Press, 1967.

Homer, *The Odyssey,* trans. A. T. Murray. Loeb Classical Library. Cambridge: Harvard Univ. Press, 1984.

———. *The Iliad of Homer,* trans. Alexander Pope. New York: Macmillan Co., 1965.

Jonas, Hans. *The Gnostic Religion.* Boston: Beacon Press, 1963.

Jones, Ernest. *The Life and Work of Sigmund Freud,* vol. 1. New York: Basic Books, 1953.

Jung, C. G. *Collected Works.* 20 vols. Princeton, N.J.: Princeton Univ. Press.

———. *Memories, Dreams, Reflections,* ed. Aniela Jaffé. New York: Random House, 1963.

———. *Nietzsche's Zarathustra,* ed. J. L. Jarrett. Princeton: Princeton Univ. Press, 1988.

Kerényi, Carl. *Eleusis.* Princeton: Princeton Univ. Press, 1967.

Lucretius. *Of the Nature of Things,* trans. W. E. Leonard. Everyman's Library. New York: E. P. Dutton and Sons, 1943.

Marlowe, Christopher. *The Tragedy of Doctor Faustus,* ed. Louis B. Wright. New York: Washington Square Press, 1959.

Meier, C. A. *Ancient Incubation and Modern Psychotherapy.* Evanston: Northwestern Univ. Press, 1967.

Melville, Herman. *Moby-Dick.* New York: Modern Library, 1926.

Murray, Gilbert. "Excursus in the Ritual Forms Preserved in Greek Tragedy," in Jane Harrison, *Themis.* London: Cambridge Univ. Press, 1927.

———. *The Rise of the Greek Epic.* London: Oxford Univ. Press, 1907.

Neumann, Erich. *The Origins and History of Consciousness.* New York: Bollingen Foundation, 1954.

Nietzsche, Friedrich. *The Birth of Tragedy* and *Mixed Opinions and Maxims,* in *Basic Writings of Nietzsche,* trans. and ed. Walter Kaufman. New York: Modern Library, Random House, 1967.

———. "Homer's Contest," in *The Portable Nietzsche,* ed. Walter Kaufman. New York: Viking Press, 1974.

Ovid. *Metamorphoses,* trans. Rolfe Humphries. Bloomington: Indiana Univ. Press, 1955.

Plato. *Laws* and *The Republic,* in *Collected Dialogues of Plato,* ed. Edith Hamilton and Huntington Cairns. New York: Pantheon, 1961.

―――. *Phaedo,* in *Plato,* trans. H. N. Fowler. Loeb Classical Library. Cambridge: Harvard Univ. Press, 1962.

―――. *The Republic* and *Phaedrus,* in *The Dialogues of Plato,* trans. B. Jowett. New York: Random House, 1937.

Plutarch. *Moralia* VII, trans. P. H. De Lacy and B. Einarson. Loeb Classical Library, Cambridge: Harvard Univ. Press, 1968.

Porphyry. *On the Cave of the Nymphs,* trans. Robert Lamberton. Barrytown, NY: Station Hill, 1983.

Proclus. *Timaeus* 3, quoted by G. R. S. Mead in *Orpheus.* London: John Watkins, 1965.

Rahner, Hugo. *Greek Myths and Christian Mystery.* New York: Biblo and Tannen, 1971.

Rank, Otto. *The Myth of the Birth of the Hero.* New York: Vintage Books, 1959.

Schopenhauer, Arthur. *The World as Will and Representation,* vol. 1, trans. E. F. J. Payne. Indian Hills, Colorado: Falcon's Wing Press, 1958.

Sophocles. *Antigone* and *Oedipus at Colonus,* trans. R. C. Jebbs in *The Complete Greek Drama I,* ed. W. J. Oates and Eugene O'Neill. New York: Random House, 1950.

―――. *Oedipus the King, Oedipus at Colonus,* and *Antigone* in *The Oedipus Plays of Sophocles,* trans. Paul Roche, New York: Penguin Books USA, 1991.

Virgil. *The Aeneid of Virgil,* trans. Rolfe Humphries. New York: Charles Scribner's Sons, 1953.

Watts, Alan. *Myth and Ritual in Christianity.* Boston: Beacon Press, 1968.

Wilhelm, Richard, trans. *The I Ching or Book of Changes,* trans. from the German by Cary F. Baynes. New York: Pantheon, 1950.

Credits

The author thanks the following publishers for permission to reprint material copyrighted or controlled by them:

Everyman's Library for the excerpt from *On the Nature of Things* by Lucretius, reproduced from the Everyman's Library edition 1943 © David Campbell Publishers Ltd.

Harvard University Press for excerpts from *Moralia* by Plutarch, reprinted by permission of the publishers and the Loeb Classical Library from Plutarch: *Moralia,* Volume VII, translated by De Lacy and Einarson, Cambridge, Mass.: Harvard University Press, 1968; for the excerpts from *The Odyssey,* reprinted by permission of the publishers and the Loeb Classical Library from Homer: *The Odyssey,* translated by A. T. Murray, Cambridge, Mass.: Harvard University Press, 1984; and for the excerpts from *The Homeric Hymns and Homerica,* reprinted by permission of the publishers and the Loeb Classical Library from *The Homeric Hymns and Homerica,* Cambridge, Mass.: Harvard University Press, 1959.

Macmillan Publishing Company for the excerpt from *The Iliad of Homer* translated by Alexander Pope, edited by Reuben A. Brower and W. H. Bond, copyright © 1965 by MacMillan Publishing Company; and for the excerpts from *The Aeneid of Virgil* translated by Rolfe Humphries, edited and with notes by Brian Wilkie, copyright © 1987 Macmillan Publishing Company, a Division of Macmillan, Inc. (Translation originally published in 1951 by Charles Scribner's Sons).

Oxford University Press for the excerpt from *The Dialogues of Plato* translated by B. Jowett, copyright 1937.

Index